Joseph E. Brown
and the Politics of Reconstruction

Southern Historical Publications No. 16

JOSEPH E. BROWN AND THE POLITICS OF RECONSTRUCTION

by
Derrell C. Roberts

THE UNIVERSITY OF ALABAMA PRESS
University, Alabama

Table of Contents

1   Early Years and Politics   1

2   The Governor and the Confederacy   11

3   End of an Era   24

4   Johnson and the Union   33

5   Radical Reconstruction   43

6   Republican   52

7   The Legal Profession and the Courts   60

8   From Radicalism to Liberalism   70

9   Rejoins the Democrats   80

10 Toward the New South   91

11 Home, Church, and Last Days   100

    Appendixes   112

    Notes   117

    Bibliography   138

    Index   153

Joseph E. Brown
and the Politics of Reconstruction

CHAPTER 1

Early Years and Politics

The spring and summer of 1865 must have been a period of soul-searching for Governor Joseph Emerson Brown of Georgia. No doubt he looked back on his phenomenal rise in politics. Each one of the political offices that he had held had been a stepping stone to the governorship. But now he was forty-four, and the political organization of which he was a part was crumbling before the United States Army. He must have pondered his own fate. He could not have known that the controversy which had surrounded his political, economic, and social life up to 1865 would be matched by the turmoil of the years remaining until his death in 1894. To understand Brown's later years and the part he played in the politics of Reconstruction, a brief look at the period before 1865 seems appropriate.

Brown's beginnings were, if not of the poorest circumstances, then certainly of the most ordinary. His ancestry was no more distinguished than that of most Americans of his day and time. But his rise in political life was spectacular, and the amount of political power he gained was amazing.

His paternal ancestors were Scotch–Irish Presbyterians who lived near Londonderry, Ireland. In the "Glorious Revolution", they supported William and Mary against James II. The Brown family came to America in 1745 and settled in Virginia. After a time, they moved to South Carolina.[1]

Like a good many other families, the Browns took part in

the American wars against England. Joseph Brown, grandfather of Joseph Emerson Brown, fought in the American Revolution, taking part in the battles at Camden and King's Mountain. Mackey Brown, the father of Joseph Emerson Brown, moved from South Carolina to Tennessee, where in the War of 1812 he served in General William Carroll's brigade under General Andrew Jackson and fought in the Battle of New Orleans.[2]

While living in East Tennessee, Mackey Brown married Sally Rice, also of Virginian antecedents. Joseph Emerson Brown was born April 15, 1821, in the Pickens District of South Carolina, where Mackey and Sally Brown had moved just before their son's birth. While Joseph Emerson Brown was still a small boy, the family moved to Gaddistown, in Union County, Georgia. There the youthful Brown worked on the family farm and attended the "rural schools" of the neighborhood until he reached the "age of nineteen."[3] In order to attend college, Brown drove a yoke of oxen that his father had given him to the Anderson District of South Carolina and traded them to a farmer for eight month's room and board. At the same time he contracted with Wesley Leverett, principal of Calhoun Academy, for his tuition on credit at that school.[4]

When the school year ended, Brown returned to Gaddistown. He decided to become a teacher, opened a three months' school, and collected enough in fees to enable him to pay what he owed Calhoun Academy. With his remaining money and a good credit rating, he was able to attend for the next two years a new academy in South Carolina, which had been established by the former principal of Calhoun Academy.[5]

He returned to Georgia and settled in Canton in January 1844 and took charge of the town academy. There he taught school in the daytime; and, at night and on Saturdays, he read law without the benefit of an instructor. Financially, the year was a profitable one, since he cleared enough to pay his school debts.[6]

During the next year, Brown spent more time reading law, for he had dropped his full-time teaching career and was tutoring the children of Doctor John W. Lewis of Canton in return for room and board. Lewis was quite impressed with Brown and apparently realized his possibilities, for he became Brown's patron and lent him enough money to attend Yale Law School.[7]

Before entering law school, Brown passed the Georgia bar examination in August 1845 for the Blue Ridge Circuit. It is said that he missed only one question on the examination and that he won the judge's compliments for his proficiency. It is also said that, later the same day, he made his maiden speech to a jury. Whatever the truth of this story, it is well-established that Brown soon became well-known for his courtroom oratory. L. N. Trammell of Dalton, a personal and political friend, said that Brown's "speeches to juries were marvels of effect. They were clear as a sunbeam. They exhausted practical sense and reason, and put his side of a case so strongly and logically that he always carried conviction."[8]

Brown entered Yale Law School in October 1845. He had no trouble with the courses and took time to attend lectures by eminent professors in other departments, such as those of Professor Benjamin Silliman in the chemistry department. He was graduated in 1846, but did not stay for commencement. He received permission to take his examinations early so that he could attend and participate in the fall session of court at Canton.[9]

His sound legal training, thorough preparation, and keen attentiveness to his task assured success in his chosen profession. Ambitious and energetic, he continued to study law both in books and in the courtroom. He was a close student of every case, even taking notes on the proceedings of all trials. For this reason among others, his practice was lucrative from the start. During his first year of practice in Canton he made $1,200, which was a good sum in those days, and soon he was making from $2,000 to $3,000 per year.[10]

In 1847, Brown married Elizabeth Gresham, the daughter of a South Carolina Baptist minister. She devoted herself to her home throughout her life. Even after Brown became politically prominent, she took little part in the social activities that his position demanded.[11]

In Brown's first venture into politics, he successfully campaigned for a seat in the state senate in 1849. Thus he began a long series of successful campaigns, which did not end until his failure to win election to the United States Senate in 1868. In this first campaign, Brown, a Democrat, was opposed by John M. Edge, a Whig, for state senator for the 41st District, which included Cherokee and Cobb counties. Brown, who was an active Baptist and a member of the "Sons of Temperance," brought the temperance issue into the campaign by refusing to buy whiskey for the voters. For this reason, his defeat was widely predicted, but he won by a rather large majority.[12]

In the Georgia senate, the main issues discussed were states rights, the new state-owned railroad (the Western & Altantic), and women's property rights. In his first term in the state senate, Brown led the Democrats in the movement that sent delegates that supported states rights to the Nashville Convention. That convention was called to meet on the issue of slavery in the newly acquired Mexican Territory, which was later settled, temporarily, by the Compromise of 1850.[13] The Western & Atlantic problem centered around the fact that the new state-owned railroad was nearing completion, but blasting through Tunnel Hill was costing a great deal of money, running up the state debt, and causing much legislative debate. Nevertheless, the work on the railroad continued until it was completed. At the same time, a bill of a domestic nature gained just as much attention as affairs of the Western & Atlantic Railroad. A. J. Miller, leader of the Whigs in the state senate, introduced the so-called Woman's Bill, aimed at legally separating the property of wives from that of their husbands. During this particular session, the Democrats, under Brown's leadership, defeated the bill, but it was passed at a later session.[14]

Alfred H. Colquitt, assistant secretary of the senate during this term, reported only two speeches from that session to his hometown paper the Macon *Telegraph,* and one of them was Brown's. This was the beginning of a long and important political relationship between the two men,[15] most of the time as allies.

In the national election of 1852, Brown advanced his career by becoming the youngest elector in Georgia. He drew more votes for the position than any other elector in Georgia, and he voted for Democrat Franklin Pierce for president. This election had some influence on him, for a son born in 1853 was named Franklin Pierce Brown.[16]

Having served as a state legislator and then as a presidential elector, Brown next won an office in the judicial branch of the state government. He was elected judge of the Blue Ridge Circuit, which included his home, Cherokee County. Superior court sessions in those days, frequently more important socially and politically than legally, sometimes became quite rowdy. Especially was this true of the Blue Ridge Circuit, which was presided over by Judge David Irwin before Brown defeated him in 1855. Brown became, despite his youth, well-known for his strictness in maintaining order in the court and in clearing the docket every term. In these respects Brown differed markedly from his predecessor. Brown enjoyed his term on the bench, and for years friends were wont to refer to him as "Judge."[17]

Two years later, in 1857, Brown's political career received an even bigger boost. The Democratic party had many likely candidates for the governorship, but Brown was not one of them. Five were prominently mentioned for the office and received votes at the nominating convention, but none of the five won the necessary two-thirds majority, and the result was a stalemate. The candidates were James Gardner, editor of the Augusta *Constitutionalist;* H. G. Lamar, a judge and congressman; John H. Lumpkin, a prominent North Georgia politician; Hiram Warner, a Northerner who came South and was, at the time, a state supreme court judge; and W. H. Stiles, a favorite of the people of Savannah, who had been plenipotentiary minister to Austria under President James K. Polk.[18]

There were too many candidates in the race for anyone to obtain a majority, and the balloting went on for three days. L. N. Trammell, long a Brown supporter, had foreseen a stalemate and devised a plan to promote Brown's nomination for governor. Before the nineteenth ballot, Trammell presented his friend's name. Brown received three votes. After the twentieth ballot, it was decided that a nomination by this convention was an impossibility, so a committee of twenty-four, three from each of the eight congressional districts, was appointed to recommend to the convention a Democratic nominee for governor.[19]

The committee decided to vote on its recommendation by secret ballot. While the process of casting the ballots was in progress, Linton Stephens moved that Joseph E. Brown be recommended by a voice vote. Brown was recommended by the committee unanimously and was then approved by the convention. Out of curiosity, the secret ballots of the committee were taken up and tabulated. It was found that had this method of recommendation been adhered to, Alfred H. Colquitt, though not previously mentioned as a candidate, would have been recommended by a majority of one vote in the committee.[20]

The American (Know-Nothing) party nominated Benjamin H. Hill to oppose Brown. The issues were mostly national ones, concerning the Kansas–Nebraska Bill and slavery in those areas, as well as President James Buchanan's administration. The Democrats endorsed the Buchanan administration but condemned Robert J. Walker, the territorial governor of Kansas, and opposed his idea of popular sovereignty for that territory. Hill and the American party also blamed Governor Walker for all the trouble in Kansas.[21]

The main issue in Georgia grew out of the controversy over the Western & Atlantic Railroad. The state-owned road, completed in 1851, had cost a great deal, and it was not yet bringing in much money. As a result, some Georgians believed that the state had a "white elephant" on its hands.[22] Therefore, members of the American party advocated the sale of the railroad, while the Democrats were for the retention of it.[23]

The campaign of 1857 was a most vigorous one. On more than one occasion, Hill, who even then was a very gifted and polished orator, outwitted Brown on the debating platform. Recognizing the threat to Brown's campaign, Howell Cobb, Robert Toombs, and other leaders of the Democratic party called a halt to the debates, and Toombs took Brown on a speaking tour of South Georgia. Toombs decided, after a time, that Brown had learned enough about public speaking to win the election. Brown learned quickly. He developed an effective style of speaking, in which he used homey phrases and pronunciations that appealed to most voters.[24] His pronunciation of the word judgment with the accent on the last syllable was a distinctive feature of his speech for the rest of his life.

The Democrats won October 5, 1857, and the American party carried only two of the eight congressional districts. The returns gave Brown the governorship of Georgia by a majority of more than two thousand votes. Although not yet thirty-seven years old, Brown was to serve four consecutive two-year terms as Georgia's chief executive.[25]

The first difficulty Brown encountered as governor was with the banks. His fight against the banks gave him the nickname "Young Hickory" since his views on banks were somewhat the same as Andrew Jackson's. They both advocated local banks with no national control. He charged the bankers with "high commercial, moral, and legal crimes." In 1857 a depression struck the country, which put a strain on banks that made strictly specie payments. Since jurisdiction over the type of payments that the banks made was in the hands of the state, those that could not obtain relief from the state governments or remain open on the basis of their former strength had to close their doors.[26]

Georgia had a law forbidding the suspension of specie payments by its banks. Even so, when the depression came, Governor Herschel V. Johnson agreed not to prosecute the violators of this act until the legislature could meet under a new governor. When Brown became governor, the legislature was asked to pass an act allowing the suspension of specie payments, thus giving relief to the Georgia banks.[27] The first session of the legislature under Brown's administration did introduce a bill suspending specie payments for a year. The bill was passed by both houses but Brown vetoed it, fully realizing that the bill would be passed over his veto, as it later was. However, as was shown by various indignation meetings, public sentiment approved Brown's veto.[28]

Brown skillfully used the bank issue as a political "whipping boy." He politically tied bankers and banks to his opposition and condemned all measures that would have made banks more powerful. Some members of the press in the state criticized his action and referred to him as a "country bumpkin." Other papers took Brown's side in the affair, as well as did a majority of the people of Georgia. Local indignation meetings were called. One at Cullouden objected to the Suspension Act and resolved: "Corporations are dangerous institutions, as they favor the interests of a few, by taking from the interests and pockets of the many." The Suspension Act was slated to expire in November 1858, but it was allowed to lapse in May.[29]

The issue of whether to continue the development of the Western & Atlantic Railroad did not die with the end of the campaign. When Brown took office, he appointed his former benefactor Dr. John W. Lewis as superintendent of the state-owned railroad. Lewis was instructed by Brown to adhere to the strictest of economies by cutting salaries to overpaid personnel and dismissing the employees who were not needed. Any employees who drank or gambled were also dismissed. This last provision led those who opposed Brown's administration to dub the road the "Cherokee Baptist Railroad" because they charged the administration with hiring only abstemious Baptists from Cherokee County.[30] Many of the men who were fired had been appointed by John H. Lumpkin, a friend of the politically powerful Howell Cobb.

But of all the economies put into practice, the one which appealed most to the public was Brown's order to collect the scrap iron along the right-of-way. The sale of this iron brought $20,000 to the state, and admiration to Brown. By 1860, the railroad was earning a half million dollars a year. By 1863, the dividends were large enough to convince the public that a railroad could be operated by the state at a profit.[31]

Brown tied his Western & Atlantic program to a public school plan. There had been two previous attempts at public education, but both were unsuccessful. Brown's philosophy on the subject is summed up in a statement in which he expressed the desire that "the children of the richest and poorest parents in the state meet in the schoolrooms on the terms of perfect equality of rights."[32] According to Brown's plans, as soon as the outstanding state railroad bonds were paid off, new bonds were to be issued in corresponding amounts for the purpose of public education. The legislature refused to approve Brown's plan, by which he had hoped to make Georgia second to none in education.[33] However, in 1858, the legislature did approve Brown's request that $100,000 each year be set aside from the railroad's earnings for public education. These funds were to be shared by the counties; and in 1860, Forsyth County was among the first to use its share to establish free schools. Then the war came, and the funds were used for the relief of soldiers' families. It was 1868 before the idea of free public education was seriously considered again.[34]

By the election year of 1859, Brown was the undisputed leader of the Democratic party in Georgia. Those who criticized him did so on the basis of the Democratic administration of President James Buchanan and the bank and the state road issues. Brown remained aloof from national affairs, and his position on the two state issues tended to win the support of the masses. To ensure a second nomination, he made a political deal with Howell Cobb whereby Cobb would support Brown for governor again; and, among other things, Brown would allow Cobb to lead a Cobb dominated delegation at the Democratic national convention in Charleston in 1860. Consequently, when the Democratic state convention met in Milledgeville on June 15, 1859, it quickly passed three resolutions: it reaffirmed faith in the Cincinnati Platform of the Democratic party in 1856, made a token endorsement of the Buchanan administration (Georgians felt that he gave up Kansas), and renominated Brown by acclamation.[35]

Meanwhile, even though the American party had dissolved, a newly formed state group, called the "Opposition party," provided an opponent for Brown. Though Benjamin H. Hill led the party, Warren Akin of Cassville, a Methodist minister and a lawyer, was its candidate for governor. Brown argued that his record stood for itself, and he refused to campaign. His health was not good; moreover, he felt that it was wise for him to stay in Milledgeville where he could look after the $35,000 to $40,000 the Western & Atlantic paid into the treasury each month. He confined his campaign to letters to newspapers and widely publicized financial reports on the state road. He defeated Akin by more than 20,000 votes.[36]

On national politics, Brown's extreme states' rights view had not changed since 1850. He was not, nor had he ever been, satisfied with the Compromise of 1850 because California was admitted as an anti-slavery state without the balance of a pro-slavery one. As a state senator, he had led the movement in the legislature that called the convention to write the Georgia Platform which accepted the Compromise of 1850 only as a last resort.[37] Between 1857 to 1860, he made it plain to Stephen A. Douglas supporters that if any part of the Kansas–Nebraska agreement was violated he would immediately call a state convention. This plan was provided for in point four of the Georgia Platform of 1850, and its obvious purpose was to discuss leaving the Union.[38] Otherwise, the most important issues to Brown were the internal affairs of Georgia.

Brown's life up to this point is well-summarized in a reply he made to a letter of congratulations on his election to the governorship in 1857: "It is true I have been very fortunate. I am in my thirty-seventh year. I was laboring on a farm and had scarcely any education at twenty. I have been very attentive to business. Whatever I have undertaken I have never failed in any enterprise."[39] One author who writes about pre-war Georgia politics describes Brown as a politician who appeared to be a "Young Hickory with a John C. Calhoun creed."[40]

CHAPTER 2

The Governor and the Confederacy

By the time the Democratic national convention met in 1860 to nominate its candidates for president, Brown led the Democratic party in Georgia. Feeling that Georgia Democrats could function independently of the national party, he was seldom concerned with efforts to appease the party's northern wing. His chief rival for state leadership of the party, Howell Cobb, was interested in the national Democratic party and with Georgia's role in it, but he got little or no cooperation from Brown.[1]

When the Georgia delegation to the Democratic national convention arrived in Charleston, South Carolina, where it met in 1860, it had already experienced a political battle. Candidates for the delegation from Georgia were split between those for Cobb and those against him. Brown and Alexander H. Stephens were among those who opposed Cobb. A compromise was worked out that enlarged the delegation and allowed both factions to be represented, but required that they vote as a unit.[2]

Brown did not go to the Charleston convention, but he was concerned about what happened there. He was not in favor of pushing a strong pro-South platform for full congressional protection of slavery in the territories. The Alabama delegation, led by William L. Yancey, walked out of the convention, and number of other delegations followed suit. Brown was not eased with this action. After the split in the Democratic ranks, he advocated that the party adopt the Cincinnati Platform of 1856 and give full recognition to the Dred Scott Decision.[3]

Lincoln had little chance of getting votes in Georgia, so the election there was a three-way race between John C. Breckinridge, John Bell, and Stephen A. Douglas. Brown favored Breckinridge, as did Toombs and other influential Georgians, because of his orthodox Southern view of slavery. The weakest of the three candidates, since Southerners did not trust him regarding slavery, was Douglas, and what support he got in the state was because his running mate, Herschel V. Johnson, was a Georgian. Benjamin H. Hill attempted to lure the supporters of Douglas and Breckinridge into Bell's camp, but his efforts did not succeed. In Georgia, Breckinridge received 51,893 votes, Bell 42,886, and Douglas 11,580. Although Breckinridge failed to get a majority, the state legislature awarded him the electoral votes.[4]

Meanwhile, the Georgia legislature had convened in the early part of November and was still in session on the day of the election. But before the outcome of the election was known, Brown asked that the legislature approve some emergency actions. He wanted a convention on secession with delegates to be elected on January 2, 1861, and he requested $1,000,000 for military preparations. State political leaders were asked to speak to the legislature on the subject. Robert Toombs and Thomas R. R. Cobb advocated immediate secession, while Alexander H. Stephens asked for delay and reasonable cooperation in such matters. Nevertheless, the legislature approved the action.[5]

On December 7, Brown wrote an open letter to the people of Georgia, in which he advocated secession. In his opinion, Lincoln would not be dangerous by himself, but as a tool in the hands of other Republicans, he could be a source of trouble. Brown contended that secession before Lincoln's inauguration would bring concessions regarding slavery questions rather than war as some people believed.[6]

When the secession convention met in Milledgeville in January, South Carolina, Mississippi, Alabama, and Florida had already seceded. This made Georgia very important to the future of the Confederacy. Brown was not a delegate to the convention but he, Howell Cobb, and some state and federal judges were given seats on the floor.[7] Brown's work at the convention was quietly done. One author describes him there as a "tall, soberly clothed, pious Governor," dressed in "rusty black, looking like a provincial and talking with an upcountry nasal twang. . . ."[8] Brown was partially responsible for showing the delegates from mountainous north Georgia the advantages of secession for their section, even though they had no slaves. He pointed out to them that if Georgia did not secede, the slaves would surely be freed, and the national government would reimburse slaveholders for the loss of their slaves. This would cost the government about $2,000,000,000 and would result in higher taxes for everyone, including those who had not owned slaves. Brown said the slaveholders would use this money to buy up the land of small farmers, and the freed slaves would compete with poor whites for land. Another alternative would be for the slaves to be relocated, which would cost even more tax money.[9]

On January 19, 1861, the convention decided to secede by a vote of 208 to 89. Some historians have held Brown, Toombs, Howell Cobb, and others responsible for Georgia's secession, in that they refused to listen to and cooperate with Alexander Stephens and Benjamin H. Hill. Others have contended that economic and psychological factors were stronger than the desire for cooperation.[10]

Governor Brown had begun military preparations for war sometime before secession. As early as 1858 he had recommended that volunteer companies be formed and commanded by the graduates of military schools. In case of war, these companies could easily be fused with other units.[11] Georgia Military Institute at Marietta was a highly regarded military school at that time, and Brown hoped that the legislature of 1860 would see the importance of the school in the light of the "perilous times" and increase its annual appropriation,[12] but they did not.

By November 17, 1860, he had taken definite steps to spend the one million dollars for military preparations voted by the legislature. For the Georgia militia, he asked for some specific supplies and "accoutrements."[13] Later in the month, he corresponded with Confederate Secretary of War John B. Floyd about more such supplies. He asked for and received samples of several types of equipment.[14] A few days later, he obtained a price list from Floyd.[15] Further action was taken along these lines by the governor on November 30, 1860 when he appointed General Paul J. Semmes as the purchasing agent for military arms.[16] Another step was taken on January 2, 1861 when Brown ordered the Georgia militia to occupy Fort Pulaski at Savannah. He immediately notified the governors of the adjacent states of his action.[17]

In further preparation, Brown proposed a plan to the Georgia General Assembly that would keep open the shipping lanes to Europe. The plan required that the state guarantee a fair return to any British company that could supply ships and operate the shipping line.[18]

But there were some men in Georgia who believed that Brown had not done as much as he could. A. W. Redding of Jamestown, Georgia was especially concerned about the repudiation of the fugitive slave laws by the state legislatures of the North. He felt that Brown had the power to retaliate, but he made no suggestions as to how the governor was to do so. Brown's policy, he said, was to "make a big smoke when there is some one who can't help seeing it but when it is sifted there will be little fire of the right kind found in it."[19]

Between January 19, 1861, when Georgia seceded, and February 8, 1861, when the Confederacy was formed, Brown took further action. Soon after secession, he entered into a controversy with Governor E. D. Morgan of New York. New York police had confiscated 200 rifles ordered by a Georgia firm. In retaliation, Brown impounded five ships owned by New York firms, which were in the harbor of Savannah. After the Confederacy was formed, the ships were released and the rifles were sent to Georgia. During the same period, Brown ordered the federal arsenal at Augusta confiscated. There were no difficulties involved in its occupation.[20]

Only after secession did Brown issue the first call for volunteers, on April 18, 1861. Students, clerks, farmers, and others answered the call almost immediately.[21] By May of 1861, Brown had organized six regiments and two battalions.[22] Furthermore, they were well-supplied with arms, which caused Robert Toombs to observe that Brown had "more guns than the whole Confederacy."[23]

While Brown was faced with the problem of secession and preparations for war, he was also involved in the gubernatorial election of 1861. The war helped him in this campaign, in which he was opposed by E. A. Nisbet. The main issue of the campaign was whether Brown should be given a third term. He conceded that a third term was not customary, but neither was the war, and he stood on the record of his second term. The press for the most part favored Nisbet because of the third term issue, while only two papers supported the governor. Even so, Brown was reelected over Nisbet by a vote of 46, 493 to 32, 802.[24]

News of Brown's election for a third term humiliated Howell Cobb "into the very dust." Because he had never liked him, he said that he could never again feel the same about any man who had voted for Brown. Cobb felt that the state had been disgraced and suggested that his family move to another state, not to return "while the miserable scratch disgraces the executive chair."[25]

During the fourth term campaign in 1863, the race was no more arduous than in 1861. Pre-election rumors suggested that either Linton Stephens or Robert Toombs would run for governor. Alexander Stephens is credited with persuading Brown to run for the fourth term. He was opposed by a former Unionist, Joshua Hill, and a Secessionist, Timothy Furlow. Brown received more votes than his opponents combined and carried both the civilian and the military ballot boxes.[26]

During the Civil War, as before, the affairs and needs of Georgia came first with Brown. In the fall of 1861, the shortage of salt was a problem (Georgia had previously imported salt from outside the South for the preservation of meat). In November of 1861, Brown ordered the confiscation of all salt being sold for over five dollars per bushel. The owners were to be paid five dollars per bushel for the confiscated salt, and speculation in the sale of salt was declared a crime.[27]

Other problems resulted from the overproduction of liquor and cotton. The distillation of liquor helped bring about a subsequent shortage of grain for food and copper for munitions. In February 1862, the governor ordered all distilleries without Confederate contracts closed. Any distillery remaining in operation was required to have a permit from Brown.[28] The next month, a proclamation was issued forbidding the use of corn in making liquor. By 1863, the legislature had outlawed the use of all foodstuff for distillation because it found that large amounts of potatoes and fruit were being used for the purpose.[29]

By 1862, oversupplies of cotton had begun to cause problems. Because of the increasingly effective blockade of the South by the Union navy, cotton supplies began to stack up in warehouses. Brown felt that Southern states should plant no more cotton than they needed for themselves.[30] He asked the state legislature to impose a heavy tax on all the cotton produced over a reasonable amount, which was to be determined on the basis of the labor available for its cultivation. "Why raise cotton," he wanted to know, "and keep it for the benefit of commercial nations after we have achieved our independence? They have left us at a critical period to take care of ourselves. Why then should we not leave them to feed their own operation till such a time when it is compatible with our public interest to produce the supply of cotton without which they must number their paupers by millions and support them by taxation?"[31] The citizens of the state responded favorably to Brown's actions; resolutions were passed in favor of them, and committees were formed to enforce them.[32]

Moreover, Brown attempted to look after the needy, especially the widows and orphans of Georgia soldiers. He gave them about $4,000 worth of corn and fodder from his own farm near Canton,[33] and he confiscated salt and gave it or sold it to them at low prices. In 1863, he asked for and got an appropriation of $5,000,000 for war relief. The legislature gave him $6,000,000 in 1864 and an equal amount in 1865. Individuals and businessmen were inspired by Brown to aid the soldiers' families. Five Georgia cotton-spinning mills offered to help families of indigent soldiers by selling them one-eighth of their output at half the market price.[34]

At the time, Georgia's fighting men were among the best equip ped, best fed, and best clothed men in the Confederacy. The Confederate army, always short of clothing supplies, appealed to Brown in August 1861, and he responded in September with a message to Georgians in which he asked for shoes and clothing for at least 30,000 soldiers.[35] As the blockade became more effective and the problem of clothing more acute, the legislature authorized the governor to seize clothing factories and manufactured goods.[36] Even by the end of 1863, when there was news of Georgia troops in need of clothing and blankets, Brown managed to get some through the blockade from Nassau.[37]

Although the militia in Georgia was better equipped than in most Southern states, it too suffered from a critical war-time shortage of munitions. The state had some arms when the war began, and it seized an additional supply from federal arsenals, but most of the confiscated materiel was given to the Confederacy. As time passed, the available supplies of arms were exhausted, and the sources from which they could be obtained were not dependable. The blockade kept European equipment out, and the Richmond, Virginia iron works were uncertain suppliers. Brown then set up various private and public projects governing the supply of arms. In May 1861, he declared that any officer who allowed his men to carry Georgia's arms out of the state would be punished. The next month he announced that the supply of arms in the state arsenal was depleted and asked the citizens to lend their arms to the state, to be paid for or returned at the end of the war. The people responded readily to his request. In 1862, the state penitentiary in Milledgeville was converted into a state armory. The prisoners there soon began to produce an average of 125 rifles per month.[38]

Another of the governor's projects was the development of "Joe Brown's pikes," of which several varieties were constructed. One hooked model could jerk the reins from the hands of enemy horsemen; another model was based on the spring and trigger principle.[39] Brown, who was very enthusiastic about the pikes, declared that the battle for Fort Donelson could have been won if the Confederacy had used them there. While "Joe Brown's pikes" were produced in large numbers in Georgia and troops were armed with them, they were never given a real battlefield test.[40]

Brown's view of Georgia's place in the Confederacy caused serious problems with the Confederate government, too. The disagreements ranged from the question of state or Confederate jurisdiction over soldiers to matters of taxation and Confederate suspension of the writ of *habeas corpus*. In the course of these disputes, there were personal conflicts between Brown and the Confederate president, Jefferson Davis.

Nevertheless, Brown pledged his support to Davis on more than one occasion. When Davis was elected for the second time in November 1861, the governor assured him that he would be "the last man in Georgia to attempt to create any division" within the Confederate government.[41] As late as 1863, Brown wrote the president that "in the main I have cordially approved of your official course and have always accorded to you high administrative ability and the most lofty patriotism." He declared further, "I shall be careful to do no act that can seriously embarrass you in the prosecution of the war, with vigor, promptness, and energy."[42] It might be well to remember that Brown was, at the time, campaigning for a fourth term as governor of Georgia.

In spite of these protestations of loyalty to the Davis government, the president must not have been surprised when Brown began to criticize, for in April 1861, Thomas R. R. Cobb had reported that "Davis holds Brown in great contempt, he says he is the only man in the seven states who had persistently thwarted him in every endeavor to carry out the policy of the government." Cobb's brother, Howell Cobb, not only remained a political enemy of Brown, but he also became a strong supporter of Davis. Apparently Davis and Cobb felt somewhat alike about Brown. In May 1861, Howell Cobb thought he saw an open break coming between the president and the governor, and he hoped to help Davis "put down the miserable demagogue who now disgraces the executive chair. . . ."[43]

Foremost among the disagreements between Davis and Brown was that of jurisdiction over troops. In the first stages of the war, Davis requisitioned troops from the states by companies.

Brown argued that Georgia should be allowed to send troops by organized regiments, which would give him the privilege of appointing regimental officers. By April 1861, he had won that phase of the argument. Then the Confederacy by-passed the state authority and began to accept men directly into the Confederate army. In some cases the men took their guns and equipment with them. Brown objected strenuously, and letters and actions of defiance began to pass between Brown and Confederate officials.[44]

In April 1862, the Confederacy passed a conscription act that brought down Brown's wrath. He argued that in view of states' rights such an act was unconstitutional, for state requisition was the only legal means of raising an army. Even more galling to Brown was the fact that as he organized state militia, subsequent conscription acts lowered and raised age limits so as to make his militia subject to conscription. This required that several devices be used to rebuild the militia. He organized county seat parades and parades of pretty girls to inspire patriotism, and when other methods proved inadequate, he instituted a draft to replenish the state militia.[45]

Brown wrote to President Davis and to Secretary of War George W. Randolph almost immediately after the conscription acts were passed. He told Davis that he did not "feel that it . . . [was] the duty of the executive of a state to employ the officers of state in the execution of a law which virtually strips the state of her constitutional military power," and he added that this would destroy the state's legislative organization. "I therefore," he concluded, "respectfully decline all connections with the proposed enrollment and propose to reserve the question of the constitutionality of the act and its binding force upon the people of this state for their consideration at a time when it may less seriously embarrass the Confederacy in the prosecution of the war."[46]

To Secretary of War Randolph, he wrote that he felt the conscription acts were not only unconstitutional but also unnecessary as far as Georgia was concerned. Nevertheless, he promised "to throw no obstacles in the way of its [conscription] being carried out in Georgia further than might become absolutely necessary to preserve intact the State government in all its departments civil and military."[47]

But there were loopholes in the conscription acts, and Brown was among the first to take advantage of them, even though he had previously objected to the substitution and exemption laws. He continued to complain that these unconstitutional acts would eventually destroy not only the state militia but the entire state government. In spite of his objections to the laws, hundreds of members of the state militia were given minor state government jobs after the Confederate government had ruled that state employees were exempt from conscription. Both inside and outside of Georgia, these exemptees were derisively dubbed "Joe Brown's Pets."[48]

By 1864, the shortage of able-bodied men for the Confederate army was obvious to Confederate officials. The problem was so acute that the Confederate congress began to advocate, and finally approved, a plan to draft Negroes into the army. Brown, and, ironically, Howell Cobb, both opposed the plan on the grounds that this was against all the principles for which the Confederacy was fighting.[49] He also opposed the practice of the impressment of slaves by the Confederate army for work details. On a number of occasions, the governor obstructed the efforts of Confederate army officers to carry out the impressment of slaves in Georgia.[50]

Throughout the war, the question of the status and jurisdiction of the state militia was not settled. Brown refused to allow state troops to leave Georgia, even though this necessitated sending more soldiers than were needed to guard the Atlantic Coast. On November 17, 1864, after the state militia had been turned over to Joseph E. Johnston and John B. Hood, he called for a "levée en masse" of all able-bodied men, regardless of age. But on December 19, 1864, he granted all members of the militia a furlough, despite the fact that federal troops were streaming into Georgia from Alabama, and Sherman was in the process of taking Savannah.[51] These and other actions by Brown prompted someone under the pseudonym "Troup" to write the Macon *Telegraph* that whenever "you meet a growling, complaining, sore-headed man, hostile to the government and denunciatory of its measures and policy, or a croaking desponding dyspeptic who sees no hope for the country, but [sees it] whipped as badly as himself, you will invariably find a friend, admirer and defender of Governor Brown."[52]

Unfortunately for the South, since it split the leadership, Brown was joined by Vice President Alexander H. Stephens and his brother, Linton Stephens, in denouncing the suspension of the writ of *habeas corpus* by the Confederacy. The trio persuaded the Georgia General Assembly to pass resolutions against the suspension of the writ, but Brown was accused of employing dubious means to persuade the general assembly to pass them.[53]

Earlier, Brown and the Stephens brothers had also objected to a financial plan of the Confederate congress whereby the Confederacy could issue bonds based on state endorsement. Brown said Georgia had managed her affairs wisely, and Georgia alone had the right to the benefits of her good credit; her funds should not be divided among the states that had not been so efficient. The only fair method of raising money for the Confederacy, thought Brown, was by taxation. Since the Confederate bond plan needed unanimous ratification by the states, it failed.[54]

The governor continued to agitate for a Confederate tax until he got the state legislature to pass a resolution demanding one. Under this and other pressures, the Confederate Congress began to discuss such an act in the fall of 1862. However, it was not until April 1863 that any kind of comprehensive tax bill was passed.[55]

In addition, Brown took exception to the confiscation of supplies by the Confederate army in Georgia, even in extreme emergencies. At the same time, he objected to federal restrictions on blockade running until the end of the war. A Georgia editor compared the governor's arguments to those of the old woman "who wants something because she wants it."[56]

It was apparent to both the Confederacy and the Union that Brown and the Stephens brothers were at odds with Jefferson Davis and his government. By the autumn of 1864, Governor Brown was paraphrasing Patrick Henry's plea for freedom from tyranny. "As for myself," he said, "give me liberty as secured in the constitution with all its guarantees, amongst which is the

sovereignty of Georgia, or give me death."[57] In a speech to the
November 1864 meeting of the Georgia General Assembly, the
Governor said that in a "crisis like the present, Statesmanship
is even more important than Generalship." "Generals," he continued, "can never stop a war, though it may last twenty years
till one has been able to conquer the other." "Statesmen terminate
wars by negotiation," he concluded.[58]

When General William T. Sherman occupied Atlanta in September 1864, he was fully aware of this rift between Brown
and Davis, and he attempted to take advantage of it. He contacted
Governor Brown and Vice President Stephens through Georgia
Unionists Joshua Hill, R. K. Wright, and William King. Sherman
wanted Georgia to withdraw from the war; in return, the general
would keep his army restricted to the public roads and pay for
what it consumed in the further invasion of the state. Robert
Toombs advised his friend Stephens not to get involved with
Sherman, and the vice president subsequently argued that
neither he nor the general had the authority to make any sort
of treaty. Brown, who was in the midst of a new struggle with
the Confederate War Department over his state militia, which
he withdrew from General John B. Hood's army, thought that
a talk with Sherman would be impractical but that Georgia still
could make peace through proper state channels.[59]

Later, in November 1864, Brown, the state legislature, and
other officials fled from Milledgeville before Sherman arrived.
The governor took his family to what is now Cordele, Georgia,
where he had bought a modest farm. The legislature, whose
session had been interrupted by Sherman, reconvened at the
Macon City Hall on February 15, 1865.[60] The governor told
the legislature that he had completely lost faith in Davis and
that he wanted a state convention called to initiate an amendment
to the Confederate constitution so as to take away the control
of the army from the president. "The night is dark," he said
despondently, "the tempest howls, the ship is lashed with turbu-
lent waves, the helmsman is steering to the whirlpool, our remon-
strances are unheeded, and we must restrain him, or the crew
must sink together submerged in irretrievable ruin."[61]

Brown's statements did not go unchallenged. Benjamin H.

Hill, a close friend and admirer of President Davis, was making some obvious allusions to Brown when he said, "And if we are conquered, subjugated, disgraced, ruined, it will all be the work of those enemies among us; and they will accomplish that work by destroying the faith of our people in their own government." In denouncing Brown, he concluded that he "dreaded the subtle power of the serpent that coils within the garden, far more than I do a million of bayonets bristling without the walls."[62] But the Confederacy was in its last days. Neither Brown's attempts to trim the power of the president nor Hill's attacks on Brown had any real effect. Brown surrendered the state militia in May 1865.

There is little doubt that Brown's policy regarding the principle of states' rights was the one for which the war was fought by the South; but in practice, this principle was not conducive to a unified war effort. Therefore, while Brown helped fight the war, in some ways he actually hindered the war effort. One noted historian has written, "Governor Brown took as much interest in managing Georgia as if it had been his farm, and throughout the war he watched over Georgia property and Georgia people with a sharpness often more zealous than wise."[63]

CHAPTER 3

End of an Era

With Lee's surrender in April 1865, an era ended in the career of Joseph Emerson Brown. He had defied state Democratic leaders on taking the reins of the governorship in 1857, he had defied the United States government in 1861, and then for four stormy years he had defied Jefferson Davis.

Circumstances and events at the end of the Civil War prohibited more defiance, Brown reasoned, and he decided to become conciliatory. At that time, he wrote to his friend Alexander H. Stephens that his future course would be based on the finality of the Confederate defeat. He would "remain in the state" and do all he could to "aid in the restoration of order and to mitigate suffering" as long as he was allowed to do so. But if he was arrested and carried off, he would meet his fate with "coolness."[1]

On April 27, the day after Johnston surrendered to Sherman, Brevet Major General J. H. Wilson, of the United States Army at Macon, asked Brown for an interview "in regard to the existing status of affairs in Georgia."[2]

Some correspondence followed between Brown and Wilson which, for the most part, dealt with the opening of the railroad between Dalton and Atlanta.[3] At Wilson's request, Brown directed the superintendent of the Western & Atlantic Railroad to aid the United States Army in any way that he could in the work of rebuilding the railroad. Further, Brown agreed to meet Wilson in Macon to talk about this and other matters.[4]

Meanwhile, news had come that Johnston had surrendered to Sherman on terms similar to those extended to Lee at Appomattox. Sherman then directed the generals under his command to negotiate with Confederates in their respective areas on precisely the same terms.[5]

Accordingly, Wilson wrote Brown on May 3, offering him the same terms given Lee and Johnston. Wilson himself would accept the surrender, for which double rolls of officers and men were to be presented; the officers must be given "individual paroles not to take up arms against the United States government until properly exchanged;" and all arms and public property were to be turned over to the United States Army. Said Wilson, "This done, each officer and man will be allowed to return to his home, not to be disturbed by the military authorities of the United States, so long as they preserve their parole and obey the laws which were in force previous to January 1, 1861, where they reside."[6]

On May 5, a day later than planned, Brown arrived in Macon to confer with Wilson.[7] As a result of this conference, Brown agreed to surrender the Georgia state militia and received his military parole as its commander-in-chief. He pledged himself not to bear arms against the United States or counsel others to do so. After this pledge was signed, Brown and the militia were allowed to go home unmolested.[8]

Brown's call for a meeting of the state legislature on the day following his military parole caused quite a stir. In his proclamation he said that recent circumstances rendered it proper that the legislature convene to provide the best means of meeting the "exigencies." He announced that the legislators must bear burdens other than political ones at the coming meeting, which was scheduled to be held at the capitol in Milledgeville on May 22, 1865. Further, he warned them that while room there was plentiful, food was quite scarce, and they must bring their own.[9]

The call was made without the consent of the federal authorities. However, Brown did communicate with President

Andrew Johnson on the subject, but he acted before a reply was forthcoming. Brown wrote Johnson that the currency had collapsed in that Confederate money and bonds were no longer negotiable and that the "great Destitution among the poor" made it "absolutely necessary that the legislature meet to supply the deficiency" and to make plans toward the restoration of "peace and order by accepting the result which the fortunes of war" had imposed. Since Wilson had no instructions from his superiors, he could not permit the assemblage of the legislature. Even so, he asked the president to order that "no force be used to prevent the meeting."[10]

Brown's telegram passed through the hands of a number of people: it went first to President Johnson; it was then sent to Secretary of War Edwin M. Stanton to answer. Stanton forwarded his answer to General Wilson in Macon, who in turn sent it to Brown. The contents were quite plain and to the point. Wilson was directed to give Brown this answer:

First. That the collapse in the currency and the great destitution of provisions among the poor of the State of Georgia mentioned in his telegram has been caused by the treason, insurrection, and rebellion against the authority, Consitution and laws of the United States, incited and carried on for at least four years by Mr. Brown and his confederate rebels and traitors, who are responsible for all the want and destitution now existing in that State.

Second. What Mr. Brown calls the result which fortunes of war have imposed upon the people of Georgia and all the misery, loss, and woe they have suffered are chargeable upon Mr. Brown and his confederate rebels who usurped the authority of the State and assuming to act as its Governor and Legislature, waged treasonable war against the United States and by means of that usurped authority protracted the war to the last extremity, until compelled by superior force to lay down their arms and accept the result which the fortunes of war have imposed upon the people of Georgia as the just penalty of the crimes of treason and rebellion.

Third. That the restoration of peace and order cannot be [sic] intrusted to rebels and traitors who destroyed the peace and trampled down the order that had existed more than a century and made Georgia a great and prosperous State. The persons who incited this war and carried it on at so great a sacrifice to the people of Georgia and the people of the United States will not be allowed to assemble at the call of their accomplice to act again as a Legislature of the State and usurp its authority and franchises. Men whose crimes have spilled so much blood of their fellow citizens, impoverished the people of Georgia, destroyed the finances, currency and credit of the State, and reduced the poor to destitution, will not be allowed to usurp legislative powers that might be employed to set on foot fresh acts of treason and rebellion. In calling them together without permission of the President, Mr. Brown perpetuated a fresh crime that will be dealt with accordingly.

Fourth. You will further inform Mr. Brown that the President of the United States will without delay exert all the lawful powers of his office to relieve the people of Georgia from destitution by delivering them from the bondage of military tyranny which armed rebels and traitors have so long imposed alike upon poor and rich.[11]

This communication, sent on May 7, at 6 P. M., was followed one hour later by an order for Brown's arrest which was sent by Stanton at the direction of the president. Brown was to be arrested "immediately" and sent under "close custody" and "under sufficient and secure guard to Major General Augur, at Washington" and he was to be allowed no communication, "verbal or written, with any person but the officer having him in charge. . . ."[12] Not only was Brown to be arrested, but Stanton also ordered that any other "prominent rebel who may take any steps toward reorganizing rebels should be seized immediately and sent to Washington under guard."[13]

Captain Kneeland of Wilson's staff was sent from Macon to Milledgeville by special train to arrest Brown.[14] Later, in writing to President Johnson about this incident, Brown said that he was "taken from his home at night on notice of 30 minutes to make . . . arrangements for . . . [the] trip to . . . prison. I presented the parole and protested against the arrest, and was informed in reply that it was the order of General Wilson that the guard take it away from me. I then surrendered it under protest. At the moment it was demanded of me I could have commanded force enough to have captured the squad sent to arrest me without the slightest difficulty and have made my escape. My determination was and is, however, to make no effort to escape."[15]

General U. S. Grant was puzzled by Brown's arrest. There

seemed to be some question as to whether Brown's call for the legislative assembly came before his parole, as Brown claimed, or after it. Said Grant, "If the call for the meeting of the Legislature was subsequent to his parole, I suppose there can be no doubt but that he stands liable for arrest for violation of his parole. Otherwise, it is not obligatory upon the Government to observe their part of the contract. I would not advise authorizing him to go back to Georgia now under any circumstances, but I do not think a paroled officer is subject to arrest so long as he observes his parole without giving him notice first that he is absolved from further observance of it."[16]

There appeared to be some doubt about Brown's arrest in Stanton's mind, too. He wrote Grant that he would "refer the question as to how far the parole operates to the Attorney-General." "It seems to me," he continued, "that his political actions, in assuming the functions of Governor, are not covered by his military parole as commander in chief of the State militia."[17] Under this interpretation, Brown would have needed two paroles, one military and the other political.

Meanwhile, Brown's legislative call had to be disposed of in some manner. This was done by Special Order No. 63, of May 15, 1865, which declared Brown's call null and void and forbade members of the Georgia legislature to meet at the appointed time and place.[18]

If the United States authorities were disturbed over Brown's call, the people of Georgia were also disturbed. The citizens of Effingham County called a mass meeting at which resolutions were passed commending Governor Brown for calling an extra session of the general assembly for the purpose of "repealing the ordinance of secession." This meeting, held late in May, was of no consequence, however, because Special Order No. 63 had already prevented the assembly from convening.[19]

While several other counties called meetings to compliment Brown on his action, there was some unfavorable comment in the Georgia press. The Savannah *Daily Herald* held that Brown was no longer governor and that Georgia had been under the direct control of the national government ever since the state surrendered. Further, Brown had been declared a traitor, and

the editor said that "traitors shall not govern." The citizens of
Georgia, he added, "must conform in all respects to their new
condition, to be a prosperous people."[20]

Relatively little is known about Brown's trip to Washington
except the facts set down by the federal officer who accompanied
him. Brown was ordered to leave Macon on May 10, the day
Jefferson Davis was captured, under a guard consisting of Lt.
William Bayard, one non-commissioned officer, and four enlisted
men.[21] On the trip, Brown rode in a wagon.[22] At Atlanta his
guards secured fresh horses and a stronger escort to Dalton.
Apparently, because this area had been Brown's home for most
of his life, they feared trouble.[23]

Leaving Chattanooga on May 13,[24] Brown reached Nashville
on the morning of May 15 and left the same afternoon.[25] There
were rumors that Brown had been seen walking down the streets
of Nashville, arm in arm with Governor Brownlow. This is
unlikely, however, unless the orders to the escort, which decreed
that Brown should not be allowed to talk to anyone, were fla-
grantly disregarded.[26]

Brown and his escort arrived in Washington on May 20. He
was placed in Carroll Prison with Governor Letcher of Virginia
and Governor Vance of North Carolina. By this time, according
to current gossip, Brown was to be called as a witness in a proposed trial of Jefferson Davis for "complicity in the assassination
of President Lincoln."[27]

On the same day that Brown reached Washington, he com-
municated with the president through the provost marshal. In
his letter to Johnson, Brown explained the circumstances of his
arrest. As to his proclamation he added, there were facts connected with it that could be explained "verbally in a much more
satisfactory manner than by . . . written communication." "I have,
therefore," he wrote, "most respectfully to ask that I be allowed
a personal interview for that purpose." In closing, Brown told
the president that General Wilson had received a notice of the
legislative call several days before the surrender and parole.[28]

Brown spent the afternoon of May 21 in the president's office
in conference with Johnson and Stanton. At the suggestion of
Stanton, Brown's account of the conference was recorded in

the form of a letter to the president.[29] In his letter, Brown attempted to explain his position on the issue of his proclamation. As he understood it, Brown said, the agreement made between General Johnston and General Sherman on April 26 called for state sovereignty, "and the present state governments were not to be disturbed." To further substantiate the report he mentioned a published story that Governor Vance was asked by federal authorities to "resume the exercise of the functions of his office and to convene the legislature of his state."[30]

Brown claimed that the financial condition of Georgia impelled the meeting of the general assembly, for there had been a complete collapse of its fiscal structure. The legislature had appropriated $8,000,000 for the relief of the poor and the families of the soldiers, which was necessitated not only by the devastation of the war but also by the depreciation of the Confederate currency. Unless relief measures were taken, there would be great suffering among the poor and anarchy might quite possibly result from it. Further, the rebellion was over. When Lee surrendered, he did so because the cause was lost, and it would be criminal to continue the war without any hope of success.[31]

Brown had not made the decision to call the legislature without advice; he had conferred on the subject with a large number of distinguished men, including several who were known to have favored the Union cause both before and during the war. All of these men, "without a single exception, urged the propriety of convening the legislature at as early a day as possible," for the purpose of putting the state back into the Union and providing relief for the poor.[32] When Brown called for the legislature to convene, he had no idea that the federal government would object to its meeting. Neither did he have any intention of advising it to continue hostilities. "I knew it [the United States government] had the power to dictate its own terms," he said," and that the people of the South had no ability to resist its will." It was the duty of the people of the South, he believed, to accept the outcome of the war and "do all in their power to restore prosperity and repose to the whole country."[33]

Brown did not deny his part in the war, but he made it plain that he had changed his position. Frankness urged, he said,

"that I state further that I was an original secessionist and an
ardent, and I trust an honest believer in the correctness of the
doctrine of that school of statesmen. But when the decision was
made against that right by the most powerful tribunal known
among nations—the sword—I felt and still feel that it is the
duty of the people of the South to yield and accept it as the
law of their conduct in the future, and do all they can in the
new state of things to repair the losses sustained by the war."[34]

Evidently, Brown's conferences and letters had the effect he
desired. In a letter to President Johnson, he pleaded: "[If] I
could be released on parole in the city, pending the investigation
of my case, it would be a great relief, and would enable me
with greater facility to prepare a point in the case that may
require my attention." On May 29, nine days after he reached
Carroll Prison, he was given a "parole of honor" by the president,
which permitted him to leave the prison during the day and
allowed him the privilege of going about Washington. He could
"pass to and from his quarters in this city without interruption. . . ."[35]

It is known that Brown had at least one more conference
with President Johnson before he was paroled on June 3.[36] His
parole, which permitted him to go back to Georgia on that date,
came exactly two weeks after his imprisonment, during nine
days of which he had been strictly confined.[37] He forthwith
notified Mrs. Brown that he would be home by June 20, and
that he would return via New York and Savannah.[38]

Even before his release, newspapers carried rumors of his
parole and their interpretations of the incident. The release,
said one paper, "is not relished much by some people, but
undoubtedly the President and Cabinet have sufficient reasons
for their leniency in this case."[39] A dispatch from New York,
dated June 1, said that in return for his freedom, Brown had
pledged "to work earnestly for the restoration of Georgia."[40]

Brown's release greatly displeased the Union soldiers who had
been confined at Andersonville Prison, for they held him responsible for the horrors of that place. Possibly they were mistaken.
An Augusta paper, for example, explained that Brown was in
no way responsible for the Andersonville tragedy. The credit

for this, the paper said, should be given to "those who had the management of affairs at Richmond"; they were "wholly and solely responsible."[41]

Brown's trip home was not without incident. After the journey from Washington to New York, he boarded the *Argo* for the voyage home. He reached Hilton Head, South Carolina, on June 15,[42] and went on to Savannah to spend a day or so with his friend David Mayer before he took the overland route to Milledgeville on June 18.[43] The trip was marred for Brown by a rather serious attack of "billious [sic] fever." Although seriously ill Brown continued the journey home after a short delay and recuperated there.[44]

This ended the Confederate era for Joseph E. Brown. Also it ended the period of defiance for him. For the next several years he attempted to conciliate his opponents and cooperate with them. He had been successful in this policy in Washington, but in the future it was to bring wrath and infamy upon him at home.

CHAPTER 4

Johnson
and the Union

After returning to Georgia with his parole in June 1865,
Brown was inactive for a short time, recuperating from his illness.
But within a month, he began to busy himself with the problems
at hand. First, he felt that he should resign from the governorship, which brought repercussions from the federal army officials
in Georgia. Then he was faced with the problems of obtaining
a full pardon from the president and participating in state political affairs (rather indirectly). To earn his livelihood, he went
back into law practice, this time in Atlanta.

Brown's return from prison pleased most people in the state.
His illness on the trip further accentuated sympathy for him.
One newspaper gave a very favorable account of his administration. Governor Brown's ambition, the paper said, was to make
Georgia "great and prosperous, in short, to make her a model
state...." Further, for the good of Georgia, Governor Brown
hoped that every Georgia citizen not excluded from political
privileges by President Johnson's proclamation would "qualify
himself and take an active part in achieving to restore our beloved
State to her former prosperity and glory." Brown, the editor
said, had many personal enemies, but "his enemies are his
enemies for the very same reasons that his friends are his friends:
on account of his virtues."[1]

On June 19, 1865, Brown resigned the governorship of Georgia. In a published statement, he thanked the people of the

state for having elected him governor for an unprecedented four terms. The South, he said, had "been overcome by superior numbers and boundless resources of the North, and we have no alternative but to accept the result." The existing state governments of the South were not recognized by the North, therefore, he was resigning the office "into the hands of the people who . . . [had] so generously conferred it upon" him. He had been arrested and released, but he had been given no pardon; he had taken no oath. Even so, he recommended that the people of Georgia give President Johnson's "administration a generous support."[2]

Ordinarily, this resignation should have made Governor Brown's enemies quite happy, but the United States Army officials in Georgia were quite disturbed over the event. General Wilson wrote from Macon to his commanding officer, General George H. Thomas: "Unless he has done this by direction and permission of the President, I think he should be arrested and removed to a Northern prison."[3] General Thomas replied he was "inclined to think that the President permitted J. E. Brown to resign as Governor. . . ." This reply ended any idea of rearresting him.[4]

During July and August, though he was still feeble from his illness, Brown traveled about the state, giving opinions and getting those of other people. He left Milledgeville in late July for his Canton farm,[5] stopping for a short time in Atlanta,[6] and on August 6, he was interviewed in Augusta by a newsman. He gave the reporter his opinion of the situation in Georgia and the United States. He hoped that Georgia people would, as he had determined to do, accept the policy of President Johnson. "The longer Georgia is antagonistic to the powers that be, the longer she [will] stay out in the cold." The president, himself, Brown concluded, would be as conciliatory toward the South "as the interests of the whole country would admit."[7]

Meanwhile, Brown had kept up a steady correspondence with President Johnson. In July, Brown telegraphed the president that no opportunity was "offered the people of many of the counties of the State to take the amnesty oath." Nevertheless, Brown thought that the backwoods people would be pleased with the national policy and that there would be no trouble in the coming state convention.[8] Three days later, on July 24, 1865, the President wired Brown that the recently appointed provisional governor, James Johnson, would have the power to appoint officials to administer the oath; meanwhile, "any military or civil officer who is loyal to the Government of the United States" could administer it.[9]

By August 7, 1865, the Brown-Johnson correspondence had become more intimate. Brown then wrote the president that it was important that "I have an interview with you about offices here. If my health will permit I should like to start to Washington in about ten days. Please send me passport...."[10] The results of this correspondence were summarized in a one line news item: "Ex-Governor Brown has gone to Washington City."[11]

Brown's trip to Washington, on which he was accompanied by Linton Stephens, did not pass without speculation by newspapers. The Augusta *Chronicle and Sentinel* had heard that the two of them had seen President Johnson in an effort to secure Alexander H. Stephens' release from prison. This paper reported that the president politely informed them that he had made no decision about releasing Stephens, but as soon as he arrived at one, he would tell them of it.[12]

Stephens' release, it appeared, was not Brown's only business in Washington. On September 5, 1865, he took the oath to "faithfully support, protect, and defend the Constitution of the United States and the union of States thereunder."[13] Following his oath, "full pardon and amnesty" were granted him because Johnson felt "his case renders him proper object of Executive clemency." The pardon also included five stipulations pertaining to the late rebellion and to slavery, and it was signed by the president and Secretary of State William H. Seward.[14] On September 6, Brown told Seward that he had "this day received the pardon of the President of the United States and hereby notify you that I accept it."[15]

Most of the Georgia press was pleased by Brown's pardon. A Milledgeville paper declared that it believed that Brown had the "confidence of the President" and added that "his pardon, at this early day abundantly proves it."[16] Meanwhile, an Atlanta paper rejoiced at this "magnanimous exhibition of clemency on the part of the Chief Executive of the Nation."[17] At the same time, a Savannah paper speculated that Brown had probably "had more interviews with the President than any man outside his Cabinet."[18] Many people believed that Stephens would soon be released to aid "Brown in the reconstruction and restoration of the State to the Union."[19] Thus, Brown was once more a citizen of the United States except for a few political disabilities, which Congress later removed.

By this time Brown had become an admirer of the President and his policies. On returning to Atlanta from Washington after he received his pardon, he expressed "the utmost confidence in the policy of President Johnson, and its ultimate triumph in Congress."[20] Later Brown stated that if there had been any vindictiveness or revenge in the president's nature or if "his mind had been cast in a smaller mould, the country would still have been drenched in blood after the battle had been hushed. . . ."[21]

At the same time, Brown may have had some influence on the president. According to a Georgia historian of the Reconstruction period:

> It is possible that ex-Governor Brown may have been one of the influences that changed Johnson from severe to moderate measures toward the rebels. Brown as one of the "plain people," not of the slave oligarchy, had qualities to appeal to President Johnson, in addition to his astuteness in dealing tactfully with the stubborn president.[22]

James Johnson was appointed provisional governor on June 17, 1865, just before Brown resigned on June 29. Under President Johnson's plan of reconstruction, the provisional governor was to call a convention to write a constitution. This convention met in Georgia on October 25 and continued until November 8, 1865. Brown, although not a member of the convention, was voted a seat in the hall.[23]

The next step after the writing of the constitution was the election of state officials. The date set was November 15, 1865. Rumors began to circulate that Brown would be a candidate for a fifth term as governor. The Columbus *Enquirer*, an anti-Brown paper, wondered if Georgia was going to "continue one man as Governor for a life-time." Commenting on this statement, a Milledgeville editor said: "If the people can get his consent to serve them as their Chief Magistrate, we have no hesitation in saying that he is our first choice for the position; and we will add, no man in Georgia can defeat him before the people."[24]

Brown, however, put a stop to all movements to nominate him for the governorship. Despite the many letters that poured in urging him to make the race, he announced that he must refuse because of his business interests.[25] An Augusta editor, who concurred in Brown's decision, declared that the ex-governor "had the satisfaction of knowing that his services were appreciated by the people." The same editor added that as for Brown's business interests, "he owes it to himself and his family, that his time be given to them"; however, he hoped that Brown would soon return to politics because "Georgia cannot afford to dispense with the services of such an able statesman."[26]

From the available candidates for the office of governor, Brown favored Charles J. Jenkins of Augusta. He publicly declared that the people should unite on one man for governor; and Jenkins, he thought, was that man. He wrote to Jenkins, "it affords me great pleasure to unite with other gentlemen who are now soliciting you to become a candidate for that important position."[27] But privately, to his friend Alexander Stephens, Brown said that he was at first quite skeptical of Jenkins' candidacy because of some of the people backing him and because of the possibility that Jenkins might dig up old party differences in making appointments. Brown's fears were allayed after "an interview . . . in which he said all I could require, and I then told him I would support him."[28] Jenkins was elected November 15.

Convention delegate J. B. Dumble of Macon believed Alexander H. Stephens failed to get the office only because the convention did not know whether or not he would accept it. O. A. Lochrane of Macon, who was to explain Stephens' stand fully, had not done so. Further, Dumble had heard many unfavorable comments concerning Jenkins. Dumble also said that "Judge

Jenkins was brought out to defeat Governor Brown" and that had they known Stephens wanted the office, Jenkins as well as Brown would have declined to run.[29]

Brown himself would have liked to see Stephens run, but he did not know how to locate him. In fact he wrote Stephens, "If I had known where a letter would reach you after your discharge [from prison at Fort Warren] I should have written you and asked your consent to the use of your name for governor, that your position in that matter might have been known at the opening of the convention. If I could then have said that you would accept the office," continued Brown, "all opposition (of which there was some) could have been silenced and your name run without opposition."[30]

Evidently Stephens' feelings were hurt and it is apparent that he blamed Brown for his failure to be elected governor. Linton, however, believed that Brown was innocent of any such intention: "Governor Brown," he said, "gave me a very full and very satisfactory account of his course at the Convention on the subject of the Governor's election. I am entirely satisfied that you have done him injustice in your thoughts on that subject." Continuing, he blamed Lochrane again for not getting to Milledgeville on time and then not clearly explaining Stephens' position on the race.[31]

Stephens' disappointment at not getting the gubernatorial office was somewhat allayed when he was elected United States senator by the legislature on January 30, 1866. In this race he had the blessings of Brown, who had written him earlier, "It is now hoped by many that you will accept the position of Senator in Congress. If so you will receive my support...."[32] Then, too, Brown had written Linton Stephens that Alexander H. Stephens was his first choice for "any place he would have."[33]

When Stephens and Herschel V. Johnson were both elected to the Senate on January 30, 1866, Brown wrote to President Johnson to explain the situation: "I wish to say in advance that the policy of electing both these gentlemen to the exclusion of both Mr. Joshua Hill and Provisional Governor Johnson did not meet with my approval." He noted that Stephens and Herschel V. Johnson were originally Union men just as Hill and James Johnson had been, but that Stephens, because he had been loyal to the South, was more acceptable to the people.[34] Evidently then, Brown opposed H. V. Johnson, because he said only one of these two men should have been elected, and Stephens was his first choice. If not, he must have had one policy for state politics and another for the national scenes, while attempting to gain favor with both. At any rate, the election was not vital, for Stephens and Johnson were never seated in the Senate.

Though Brown had been pardoned and was quite active in state politics, he was not yet completely cleared of all wartime suspicions. There had been, and continued to be, numerous criticisms of his financial administration of the state while he was governor. Consequently, the constitutional convention appointed a committee of investigation composed of Thomas P. Saffold, Charles L. Jordan, and O. A. Lochrane.[35]

Various official and unofficial charges were brought against Brown's administration, especially with reference to Brown's financial dealings with certain individuals in England. While the committee was in session, E. Starnes of Augusta, wrote Governor Jenkins that one of the Waitzfelders[36] had consulted the Starnes law firm with reference "to a claim which he has in England, upon which Governor Brown during his administration drew a bill in favor of his sons who have a house in Liverpool...." And, Starnes added, if the governor needed an attorney to look into the matter, he would be more than glad to accept the commission.[37]

One incident that was investigated by the committee was a charge reportedly made by John E. Ward, just back from Liverpool, that he had seen a letter from Brown to authorities there. There were rumors that this letter ordered certain funds standing to the credit of the state be transferred to Brown's personal credit. But Ward told the committee that he "never saw a letter from Governor Brown while in Europe, and except from hearsay... [knew] nothing about his transactions, either in his individual capacity, or as Governor of Georgia."[38]

The results of the investigation, which were made public on February 22, 1866, must have been gratifying to Brown. In part,

said the committee, "Our conclusion is, after the most rigid
scrutiny into public and private affairs of officers, from Governor
Brown down, that not one of these rumors has been sustained
by the slightest proof. Instead of fortunes having been made
by them, we find them generally poorer than when they went
into office."[39] The seventy-two page report was fifty-four days
in the making. One newspaper said the report was "full and
complete, and acquits the late State government of every charge
made against it."[40]

Brown not only took an interest in finance and politics, but
he was also concerned about local affairs. One of the biggest
questions of the day was the freedman's social and political status
in the South. The trend was toward either official or unofficial
"black codes" to govern the Negroes. Before the Georgia legislature met to consider the "black codes" and the Negro question,
a number of the legislators wrote Brown to ask his opinion on
the status of the Negro. He indicated that he was pleased to
reply to their letters. In the first place, he said, the "late war
has caused a complete revolution in our labor system in the
Southern states, and an entire change in the relations which
the white and black races occupy toward each other. The fact
is undeniable that those who were our slaves prior to the war
are now free; and so far as legal rights are concerned, are placed
upon terms of equality with us." Even so, continued Brown,
"I did not say that the negroes are equals of the white race.
God did not make them so; and man can never change the
status which the Creator assigned to them. . . . Unless madness
rules the hour, they will never be placed upon a basis of political
equality with us." This being true, the state would not be "permitted by the Government of the United States to enact one
code of laws for the white race and another for the negro
race. . . ." Brown still felt, nevertheless, that the Negro should
not be allowed to serve on juries or to vote, even though he
must have all other rights, such as suing and being sued and
testifying in the courts. Brown went on to reiterate, "I think
it unwise and injudicious for the legislature to pass any 'Freedman's code' or any other law that discriminates between the
two races, so far as rights and remedies in our courts are con-

cerned."[41] This course suggested by Brown was, in the main, the one followed by the legislature concerning the black codes.[42]

Brown's political ventures were purely indirect after the war until 1867, and they brought him no money; consequently, he went back into the practice of law. He opened a law office in the fast rebuilding railroad city of Atlanta, where he bought a large amount of land.

The most noted legal case that came to Brown during this period involved William Law, a Savannah lawyer for over forty years. The Test Oath Act of 1862 was supplemented in January 1865 so as to require that former Confederate lawyers practicing in federal courts must take the "Iron Clad Oath." Law, who had served a short time as a minor court official during the Confederacy, was therefore barred from practice in 1866 by the Test Oath Act.

As William Law's chief counsel in the United States district court at Savannah, Brown prepared a strong case. He wrote to Stephens asking for information on a similar case tried before the United States Supreme Court—exparte Garland. Subsequently, Brown used a plea similar to the one that was used in Garland's behalf.[43] He argued before Judge John Erskine that William Law had practiced in the courts of Savannah for over forty years, during which time he had committed no treason, had not been indicted by a grand jury, nor tried by a petit jury. A lawyer's admission to practice Brown compared to and defined as "property." Further he held that in this case the Test Oath Act was being invoked to serve as an ex post facto law and as a bill of attainder—both of which, he asserted, were specifically prohibited in the Bill of Rights of the United States Constitution.[44]

The district attorney who opposed Brown was Henry S. Fitch, the son of one of the senators from Indiana. Fitch's whole argument was based on what he called Aaron Burr's definition of the Law of Nations: "whatever is boldly asserted and successfully maintained." After Fitch had expounded the idea that the late war had changed the interpretation of the United States Constitution, he concluded with a somber warning, "See to it ye Senators and Representatives, that no like harm comes to this republic—

there is a sanctity and a sovereignty in the edict [Test Oath] that no court should treat lightly."[45]

Brown predicted a favorable decision in the case in a letter to A. H. Stephens, who had said he liked Brown's argument.[46] As Brown expected, Judge John Erskine found that "the act of Congress, approved January twenty-fourth, eighteen hundred and sixty-five [the Test Oath Act], so far as it was intended to apply to this case, is repugnant to the Constitution of the United States."[47]

This period, from June 1865 to February 1866, was quite a successful one for Brown. He had received his pardon, he was still active in politics, and he was carrying on a successful law practice. He had lost little or none of his popularity, but despite his successes, infamy was coming.

CHAPTER 5

Radical Reconstruction

In the light of Brown's previous acts and policies, his stand on Reconstruction might well have been predicted. On returning from imprisonment in Washington, he had resigned the governorship and counseled acquiescence in the policy of President Johnson's administration. His main contention was that the South had been defeated too severely to rise again soon and that Southerners must obey the laws of the government that had the power to enforce them. By 1867, Congress had gained control over the president by overriding his vetoes, and Brown now recognized this fact. Between March 1867 and March 1868, Congress instituted its own Reconstruction plan, which called for the military occupation of the South.

Meanwhile, early in February 1867, accompanied by Judge Dawson Walker, Brown made a trip to Washington. While they were there, the Reconstruction measures were pending. At the same time, impeachment proceedings were about to be started against President Johnson.[1]

While Brown was in Washington, he championed the opinions of the Southern conservatives in an interview with a New York *Herald* correspondent. The Reconstruction acts would make the freedman the political master of his former owner, he said, and the constitutional amendment would disqualify so many intelligent people that the irresponsible would rule and probably bring about anarchy.[2]

Upon his return from Washington, he found a letter from a group of Atlanta businessmen, including A. K. Seago and E. Hulbert, asking for his opinion on the Southern political situation. Brown counseled acquiescence in the unpopular measures of Reconstruction. This advice was to mark a turning point in his career.[3]

The general situation looked ominous to him: "The night is dark, dreary, gloomy, no rainbow of hope spans the blank impenetrable cloud that overshadows us." He and Judge Walker had talked freely with people high up in all branches of the government in Washington, and he had learned the true situation from them. Consequently, Brown concluded, "The party usually designated as the 'Radical Party' is sustained by the majority of the people of the North." At the same time, he felt that the "Democratic party is not sustained by the people and is not gaining ground" and that the "reconstruction policy of the President is not sustained by the popular sentiment of the northern people."[4]

The right of freedmen to vote had been decided already. The question at hand was the right of former Confederates, like himself, to vote. Apart from the franchise, Brown indicated that the Negroes ought not to pose a serious problem. The South should remember, he said, "in yielding to an inevitable necessity, that these people were raised among us and naturally sympathize with us. Their conduct during the war proved this." If Southerners "treat them kindly, pay their wages promptly, and in all respects deal justly with them, we shall seldom have cause to complain of their refusal to respect our wishes, or consult our wishes at the ballot box."[5]

The question of secession, Brown believed, had been settled; everyone should admit that the Southern people were again citizens of the United States. "As we live under it [The United States government]," he said, "we should look to it as the government of our choice. . . . Its flag is now our flag, its credits our credits, and we should determine, come what may, to forget the past, and defend and sustain both with all our ability in the future." The South should begin a "new era" by developing its resources. He recommended that Georgians welcome foreigners and Northerners because they would bring wealth to add to the resources of Georgia.[6]

If the South refused to ratify the Fourteenth Amendment, Brown feared the worst. Continued obstacles thrown in the way of Reconstruction by the South could bring the loss of the franchise to a larger number of Southerners. Eventually there might even be a movement to confiscate Southern property, he said. The membership of Congress who would favor such a drastic measure was not a large bloc "at present, but if we [Southerners] continue to reject the terms proposed by Congress, it is believed, it will grow rapidly in popular favor in the Northern States, and that politicians now disposed to be more moderate will be obligated to bend to the storm."[7]

Brown offered this advice:

I answer, "Agree with thine adversary quickly." We are prostrate and powerless. We can offer no further resistance. The conquerors dictate their own terms which are heightened in severity by the delay of the conquered to accept them. And above all, if peace, quiet, and returning prosperity can be restored to our unhappy country by the sacrifice, we should make it without further hesitation or delay.[8]

"We shall never get better terms," he added. Let "us comply with them and be ready to be represented in the next Congress as soon as possible."[9]

The appearance of this letter caused widespread discussion. In Milledgeville, where Brown had been quite popular, as well as elsewhere, comment on his policy was, for the most part, unfavorable.[10] Even the Milledgeville *Federal Union,* usually a supporter of Brown, published a mild rebuke. It considered Brown "one of our wisest statesmen, and purest patriots, and all advice coming from him, claims our profound respect and earnest consideration." But, said the editor, "we confess we cannot see, with the lights before us, how our situation will be improved by following his advice."[11] An Augusta editor thought Brown's policies of 1867 quite inconsistent with those of 1861 and said that the South should avoid "indecent haste" and "await vents and deal with them as they present themselves." As for

Brown's letter, the editor said he would postpone criticism and would "positively refuse to fly into a passion or display the proprieties of satire."[12]

At the same time, Brown was not without support. The Atlanta *Intelligencer* carried an editorial deploring the "motives attributed to Governor Brown," after the life of service that he had given to Georgia.[13] A letter to the editor of the same paper, signed "Georgia," thought that the people should certainly listen to the ex-governor and that they should demand that the legislature call a convention and adopt the "required Constitution."[14] Meanwhile, a meeting was held in Thomasville, Georgia, to support Brown's policy of acquiescence.[15]

Meanwhile, with the adverse criticism heaped upon him for his stand, Brown maintained that he "acted from a conscientious conviction of duty" and that he "had no doubt that it was best for both North and South that this vexed question be forever settled, and as speedily as possible."[16]

Nor did he refrain from speaking at various places when he was asked to do so. At Savannah on April 18, 1867, he told the audience that he had come before them "with no wish to please your fancy, excite your passions, or arouse your prejudices," but that he had come to "ask if we can reason together" concerning Reconstruction. Then Brown reprimanded Governor Jenkins for instituting court proceedings against the secretary of war and General U. S. Grant in an attempt to have military Reconstruction declared unconstitutional. Brown maintained that there were enough cases on the Supreme Court docket to last for two years and that by the time the court could act, Congress would have enacted and carried out Reconstruction measures.

The Confederate army had accepted the terms of its conquerors and other Southerners should do likewise. Brown advised all men of age, white and black, to register as soon as possible "and on election day [to] vote for a convention and the best men as delegates—moderate, just men—who will comply with the requirements of Congress, and make for us the best state constitution in their power." In closing, Brown said that his motto was "action, reconstruction and relief."[17]

Speaking in Milledgeville on June 6, 1867, Brown argued that Congress had pledged to readmit the states when they had complied with the Reconstruction acts. He said that if this were done, the South would control twenty senators and about eighty members of Congress, a number sufficient to make itself a force that could be heard. On the other hand, if the South rejected the Reconstruction acts, it could expect the Radicals to change the terms of the acts to satisfy themselves. But, in the meantime, if property should be confiscated in the South, the Negroes could expect no gain from it because it would be sold to pay the heavy national debt.[18]

Robert Toombs, now back in Georgia after his European exile, became disgusted with Brown over Reconstruction and broke with him. The break lasted for the rest of their lives. In writing to A. H. Stephens about the Milledgeville speech, Toombs said: "I see Brown is still speaking the same old story in his capital, to wit, that it will be 'worser for us unless we give in quickly' and he plays upon a harp of a thousand strings."[19]

While he was being criticized in Georgia, Brown made some friends among Northern newsmen. After an interview with him, a Cincinnati reporter was moved to write: "One Brown is worth to the South and to the nation more than a million Hunnicutts or Honeypots, or whatever that crazy Virginia devil's name may be.[20] He is worth more than a standing army, or a dozen acts of Congress; and he is as good a Union man today as there is in the United States. No mistake about that."[21]

Most white Georgians disapproved of Brown's suggestions in regard to Reconstruction, but it remained for Benjamin H. Hill to focus the hatred of the public upon him. Hill was a former gubernatorial opponent of Brown and with his scathing tongue and pen, he called attention to loopholes and poor arguments in Brown's writings and speeches. For the next three years, Hill was the leader and spokesman of the anti-Brown and anti-Reconstruction faction in Georgia. This faction, though large in number, was small in political influence because many of its members were disqualified as voters by the Reconstruction acts.

Hill's "Notes on the Situation" appeared in the Augusta *Chronicle and Sentinel* from June 19 to August 1, 1867, and they were described later by Henry W. Grady as the "profoundest and most eloquent political essays ever penned by an American."[22] In the first of his "Notes" Hill described Brown as one of those who had "urged us into secession as the only peaceful method of securing our rights; who afterwards led us to subjugation as the only method of escaping military despotism; [who were] now boasting of the great confidence heretofore reposed in their counsel, and advising us to accept the proposed terms for a new Union."[23]

In another "Note," Hill described Brown as only an ambitious politician "who had determined to support these measures, because they are proposed by the strong part. . . ." He cared not for the sufferings of the people, he cared only that "he may reap and rule." This person, Hill said, could not be trusted as he "was a traitor to the Union, a traitor to the Confederacy and would sell the honor of the people who trusted him—all for greed and place—first, from his own people, and then from his people's 'oppressors'."[24]

Hill wrote, too, of Brown's first meeting with General John B. Pope. On April 1, 1867, Pope was put in command of the Third Military District, which included Georgia. It was generally known that Brown met him at the train, and that night at a banquet in the general's honor, he responded to a toast to the General. Hill commented that he did not know General Pope, "but if . . . he possesses the ordinary instincts of honor that belong to an American gentleman, he must have felt an almost nauseating pity for the poor men who gathered about him in Atlanta, and forgetting the history of their fathers and the character of our institutions, welcomed in feasting and rejoicing, the inauguration of military despotism."[25]

Hill's letters had a tremendous effect on the thinking of the people, but the Milledgeville *Federal Union,* though displeased with Brown's stand, stood by him for a while longer. A letter to the editor in that paper signed "Farmerboy" stated that "God Almighty had made Joe Brown a wise man—his enemies—[had] made him a popular man, and if Joe Brown had made himself a rich man, I'm only sorry more of us ain't in his fix."[26]

Meanwhile, Brown did not allow Hill's letters to go unanswered. His "Review of Notes on the Situation" appeared in the *Daily Chronicle and Sentinel* from August 1 to August 9, 1867. The editor of that paper hesitated to publish Brown's first letter and wrote a short preface to it, explaining that the *Chronicle* wholeheartedly supported the views of Hill, Jenkins, A. H. Stephens and their adherents; nevertheless, at Brown's request, he was willing to open his columns to the ex-governor in order to give him a chance to redeem himself. But even "in confessing to chagrin and mortification upon the appearance of Governor Brown's first article . . . [the editor said that he] did not wish to be understood as forestalling public opinion against the series."[27]

Brown began his rebuttal by attempting to show Hill's inconsistencies. Hill started out as a Democrat but became a member of the Know-Nothing Party. In 1855, he was defeated for Congress on its ticket. In 1857, on the same party ticket, he lost to Brown in the race for governor. These facts, Brown thought, might have some bearing upon Hill's "Notes." By 1859, Brown continued, Hill was for secession in the event that a Republican became president; but when the secession convention came in 1861, he was elected to the convention as a Unionist or Cooperationist; nevertheless, at the convention, he voted to secede. When this same convention elected him to the Confederate congress, he began to predict "no war." In Congress, Hill voted against the Conscription Act; then later, he severely castigated Brown for his opposition to that measure. Later, Brown said, when those not subject to conscription were organized, Hill made a patriotic speech in favor of the militia and allowed his name to be enrolled. Then, when that group was called for duty, he did not go with them because he was a Confederate senator, therefore, it would be unconstitutional for him to draw a private's salary, too. This led Brown to remark: "It may be in view of the above incident in his life, that Mr. Hill exclaims in number 14 of his notes, 'I never felt I made war on the Union.' "[28]

Brown regarded the question of congressional Reconstruction as unimportant because he said that it mattered "very little which department of the government exercises the power over us"; the people should remember that the "President undertook to exercise it, and destroyed our old government, and set aside our old constitution and dictated the terms upon which we were to form new ones." Afterwards, Congress decided to direct Reconstruction in the South; and, consequently, created an unfortunate controversy. Hence Brown maintained that it "follows as we are subject to the will of the conqueror, and Congress wields the power of the conqueror, that we are subject to the will of Congress."[29]

Hill had very bitterly opposed the approaching convention to write Georgia's second Reconstruction constitution, and he advocated that the proposed convention be voted down. Brown predicted what he thought would happen if Georgia adopted such a course. The state, he declared, "would be reconstructed within two years anyway, with representatives in Congress. But the great mass of the white people and those who voted against the convention would not be allowed to vote...."[30]

Despite the opposition of Hill and other Georgia conservatives, a constitutional convention was called to write a new constitution for the state that would satisfy the Radicals and perpetuate their power. The convention, which met from December 1867 to March 1868, was made up mostly of Radicals and Negroes. While Brown was not a member of the convention, he is given credit for directing its work from backstage. In January 1868, he took advantage of an opportunity to indicate to them how he felt about Radical Reconstruction. He told the convention that he favored a constitution in keeping with the Reconstruction acts, which would give the franchise to the Negroes as well as the whites. He added that he also favored the adoption of the Fourteenth Amendment. If the convention went further in Reconstruction than Congress required, he pointed out, it would deserve the rebuke that it was certain to get. Congress had not yet given the Negroes the right to hold office, and Brown advised the convention not to attempt it, though it might come later.[31] Brown also said that he would never agree to a state constitution which would disfranchise him or any segment of the white race because of support of the Confederacy.[32]

The period beginning in February 1867 was the lowest point in Brown's political career. During the time from 1857 to 1865, he was, first and foremost, a politician; but between 1865 and 1867, he gradually lost interest in politics. However, politics were not wholly forgotten by him. He surely knew in 1867, when he proclaimed the Reconstruction policy as the one in which he believed, that it was not a popular thing to do. He must have known, too, that he would not derive any political gain from it. For if he did profit politically from his support of that policy, at the end of the Reconstruction, the conservatives would surely overthrow him.

Apparently, his support of the federal Reconstruction policy arose from his vested interest in Georgia real estate. Even before the war was over, Brown had begun to buy farms in South Georgia, real estate in Fulton and DeKalb counties, and land in the northwest part of the State. As long as Georgia was in a state of economic depression, this property and its products would be worth little. Georgia and the South would remain in the state of depression as long as Reconstruction was taking place. The quickest way to end Reconstruction was acquiescence; therefore, Brown advocated it.

Throughout this period, he asked the Southerners to welcome Northern and foreign men and money. He talked about a "new era" for the South, in which it would forget the past; and he devoted a great deal of time to defeating the proposal to confiscate Southern property—a proposal that he greatly feared. The results of Reconstruction, he always contended, would be peace and prosperity. This indicated that his primary interest was in economic gain for the South, which would certainly help him. At the same time, any incidental political power that accrued to him as a result of his Reconstruction policy would be welcomed. His Reconstruction stand was a gamble politically; but it was economically a safe stand, for Brown seldom gambled with his money.

CHAPTER 6

Republican

Brown's unpopular stand on Reconstruction brought him the scorn of the Southern conservatives and the wrath of Benjamin H. Hill. But it also brought about the removal of the remaining political disabilities placed on him by the Republicans in 1865. This was followed closely by his own identification with the Republican party. He helped to elect a Republican governor of the state, he ran as a Republican for the U. S. Senate, and he made more public statements about Reconstruction.

On March 15, 1867, less than a month after Brown had written his fateful letter on Reconstruction, Senator John Sherman of Ohio introduced a resolution "to relieve . . . Joseph E. Brown from disability to hold office."[1] A South Georgia newspaper stated that "we suppose this is what Joseph saw when he was taken up into that exceeding high mountain on the occasion of his recent visit to Washington." But it could have been worse, the editor said, for "we had rather have him for governor than [G.W.] Ashburn."[2] On July 1, 1868, an Augusta paper announced Brown's final relief and lamented: "Nothing like the luck of a lousy calf."[3]

Meanwhile, early in 1868, a Republican editor thought that the rumor that Brown would join the Democratic party was slanderous.[4] And, as most people expected, Brown joined the Republican party, which he preferred to call the "Reconstruction" party. In a speech at Rome, Georgia, on April 10,

1868, he gave his reasons for his new allegiance. His decision, he said, was made on the basis of the fact that the Democratic party of 1868 was not the old "States Rights Party" that he had once embraced. "This," he said, "was the doctrine of the Virginia and Kentucky Resolutions [written by Thomas Jefferson and James Madison] which were the textbooks of the Democratic party." "But," he continued, "this is no part of the creed of the present so-called Democracy of Georgia."[5]

At the state Republican convention on March 11, 1868, he attempted a further justification of his adherence to the Republican party. He pointed out again that he had been a "States Rights Democrat." The issue had changed and the states' rights principle of the Democratic party had dissolved. "The war," he said, "has settled these issues against us, and they can never be practically revived."[6]

Brown soon earned the universal denunciation of the conservative South by his actions at the Republican national convention, which met in Chicago on May 20, 1868. Its temporary chairman, Carl Schurz, appointed him as one of a committee of two to escort the permanent chairman to the platform. Then, while the convention was waiting for the committee on credentials to report, Thomas W. Conway, a Republican from Louisiana, suggested that Brown address the convention.

Brown, who called himself a "reconstructed rebel," began by presenting the convention with his views on the causes of the Civil War. This was unusual, for he seldom reminisced about the war since he had "little or no taste for brooding over the terrible conflict."[7] The failure of the United States Supreme Court, Brown declared, had been a large factor in bringing on the war. Its decisions, which were neither respected nor enforced, became useless. But the court was not entirely to blame. The great statesmen, Clay, Calhoun, and Webster were all dead: "When the storm arose, there was no one to pour oil on the troubled waters." Secession was the result.[8]

Next he gave the convention a short history of the Civil War, in which he emphasized his personal conflict with President Jefferson Davis. He concluded his synopsis with this statement: "But we went through the struggle—and at the end of the

struggle I had sense enough to know that I was whipped."⁹
He also pointed out that after the war was over, and he had
been released from prison, all the ports were open. Had he
so desired, he could have fled the country. But, he continued,
"I still loved my native land the best. With your construction
of the constitution established by the sword I still preferred
the government of the United States to any other recognized
government."¹⁰

Brown stated that he had first acquiesced in Reconstruction
under President Andrew Johnson's plan. Johnson had required
provisional governors to call constitutional conventions and
reconstruct states under his guidelines. Then, when he found
that Congress had gained supremacy, he again pledged to support the Reconstruction measures enacted by that body including
military occupation and rule, even though it was the unpopular
thing to do. As to his future intentions, Brown proclaimed,
"When I fought you, I fought you openly and boldly. When
I surrendered, I surrendered in good faith. When I took the
amnesty oath, I took it intending religiously to observe it." And,
in closing, he said, "Give us what we have won, and we will
succeed in this contest, and roll up a majority for General Grant
in November next."¹¹

This speech by Brown brought national attention. The *Anzeiger
des Westen,* a German language paper published in St. Louis,
Missouri, called it a "sorghum sop oration."¹² Meanwhile, the
editor of the Louisville (Kentucky) *Journal* commented on
Brown's statement that he had been a secessionist: "He wasn't,
however, honest enough to confess that he would always have
remained a secessionist if he had not seen that he could have
no hope of riding into office except upon the shoulders of the
Negroes and white 'scalawags'."¹³

An Atlanta editor lamented that the Radicals were outraged
because Wade Hampton, among others, had taken part in the
Democratic convention at New York; but, said the editor, "they
have not a word to say about Joe Brown and other traitors who
figured in the Chicago Convention."¹⁴ At the Chicago convention, the Republicans had nominated General U. S. Grant as
president to oppose the Democratic nominee, Horatio Seymour.

Brown had been an admirer of Grant for some time. During the course of his plea in the Test Oath case in 1866, he had spoken of the "magnanimity" of the general in regard to the peace terms. He had noted that Grant had said, "you are not conquered, but overpowered by superior numbers and resources." "And in this connection," Brown added, "excuse me for saying in this place, that the Southern people owe a debt of gratitude to General Grant for the firmness with which he stood by the terms of the capitulation; the liberality which has characterized his whole conduct since that time; and the many acts of kindness which he has performed for Southern men in adversity and distress."[15]

Despite his great admiration for General Grant, Brown did not actively campaign for him, probably because he was too busy with state politics. However, he did make at least one speech in Grant's favor. In it he accused the Democratic candidates Horatio Seymour and Francis P. Blair, Jr. of counseling the resumption of hostilities and went on to point out that if Grant were elected, no such event would take place.[16] Grant was defeated in Georgia, and his defeat there may have been one cause of still another Reconstruction of the state in 1869.

Brown played an active part in the governor's race in April 1868. He went to the Republican state convention, where he gave his initial support to Judge Dawson Walker. Brown soon saw that Walker was not strong enough to win the nomination; therefore, he came out for Rufus Bullock and explained his decision by saying that the convention "decided that Colonel Bullock was the best man and nominated him, and I felt it my duty to acquiesce in the decision."[17]

At the same convention, he directed part of his speech to the freed Negroes. He told them that he realized that he was no particular favorite of theirs, but that both he and they had the good of the state in common and that Bullock was the best candidate for all races. Brown predicted to the Negroes that, "Colonel Bullock will do you justice. This should satisfy you." He warned them of "unscrupulous men" who would "cheat them out of their votes" and urged them to be cautious and to "act upon the advice of those known to be their friends."[18]

In a speech at Marietta, Georgia, Brown described Bullock as a "strong Union man during the war" and predicted that Bullock, if elected, would "move off smoothly and harmoniously in accord with the Federal Government." Another reason to favor Bullock, probably the strongest, Brown said, was that "we are now seeking peace, I think it is best that we do nothing to irritate."[19]

Meanwhile, before the election, which was set for April 20, Brown was accused of all kinds of political chicanery. He was first shouldered with the responsibility for having Judge David Irwin, the Democratic candidate, removed from the governor's race. Though Irwin had always been a Union man, he had served as a district attorney in the Confederacy, and for this reason, General George G. Meade, now military commander of Reconstruction district number three, had ruled him ineligible to run for governor.[20] General John B. Gordon was then nominated by the Democrats to make the race, and though Brown supported Bullock, he had nothing to say against Gordon.

The newspapers assigned various reasons for Brown's support of Bullock in the governor's race. One editor said that Brown hoped "to be elected Senator, and to sell his five-story building at a heavy profit."[21] The same editor predicted "if Bullock is elected, Joseph Brown, an infinitely worse man than [Tennesseean William G.] Brownlow, will be Governor of Georgia."[22]

Georgia Republicans were much more successful in the state election in April, in which Bullock received a majority of 7,171 votes, than they were in the general election in November, 1868, in which Grant was defeated by Seymour in Georgia. Meanwhile, Bullock was appointed to serve as provisional governor before his elective term could begin and until the civil government of Georgia could be formed after the meeting of the legislature.[23] When Bullock was inaugurated in July, 1868, a newspaper reporter said, "Brown glowed as if he were reliving his own inauguration."[24]

Upon the formation of the civil government of Georgia, one of the first duties of the general assembly was to elect two United States senators as prescribed by the United States Constitution at that time. Since the Republicans had been successful in getting

Bullock elected, Brown decided to run for the Senate. According to a rumor circulated in Atlanta, Brown had told Democratic leaders that, in exchange for their support, he would be willing to run for the Senate with a Democrat for the other Senate post. At the same time, he would guarantee that no Democrat in the general assembly would be unseated.[25]

In the Radical caucus, held late in July, Brown was nominated for the long term in the Senate while Foster Blodgett, an Augusta "scalawag," was nominated for the short term.[26] Meanwhile, Governor Bullock was supposedly working for Brown and Blodgett. It was rumored in Atlanta that he had promised judgeships to at least four Democratic members of the general assembly on condition that they would vote for the Radical candidates. The rumor further reported that Bullock threatened to remove a judge in Glynn County unless he persuaded the representative of that county to vote for the Radicals.[27]

The campaign was a hectic one for Brown. Howell Cobb, for one, loosed his wrath on him in spite of the rumor that every speech that Cobb made gave Brown six more votes. Naturally, Cobb was most critical of Brown's Reconstruction policy. He felt that not only should Georgians not elect Brown senator, but also they should avoid any kind of relation with him. For Cobb explained, "when I see a white man talking to Joe Brown and that class of men, a feeling of revulsion comes over me. I can't help it. But when I see them talking to a negro, I feel sorry for the negro."[28]

Brown's major campaign speech in behalf of his candidacy for the Senate was interrupted by a disturbance. On the night before the general assembly began the balloting, when he spoke at Davis Hall in Atlanta, his speech was interrupted by a group of men around the door who intermittently hooted and yelled at him throughout the meeting. No amount of pleading could stop the hecklers, but no serious violence resulted from the noise they made. Finally, as Brown entered his carriage to go home, the unruly crowd gave three groans for him.[29]

On the first ballots Brown led, trailed by Alexander H. Stephens and Joshua Hill. But Brown failed to receive the necessary majority, for it was apparent that he and Blodgett were unacceptable to the Democrats, as well as to a large segment of the Republicans. Since the moderate Republicans and the Democrats were unable to change the course of the balloting, they combined to elect Joshua Hill over Brown, 111 votes to 93, and Dr. H. V. M. Miller of Atlanta over Blodgett.[30]

The city of Atlanta began celebrating Brown's defeat immediately. The crowd in the legislative chambers and that outside combined and marched through the streets singing "Glory Hallelujah." The march wound up at the United States Hotel, where the successful candidates, among others, addressed the crowd. At the end of the speeches, the crowds dispersed; but as they left, one group was heard singing "Old Brown is dead and we will hang his carcass to a sour apple tree."[31]

Robert Toombs confided his pleasure at Brown's defeat to his friend Alexander H. Stephens. There was, according to Toombs, "political justice in making the earliest traitor defeat the worst one and break down his party." Toombs thought Brown's defeat was most fortunate. Brown had the power of all Bullock's patronage, and if that of the Senate had been added, he would have become invincible. Toombs had no particular admiration for Hill, the Morgan County Unionist, for he was a weak person. But, said Toombs, "I did my utmost to elect him and ask of him no other favor than not to join us or speak to me." With regard to Brown, he felt it "was about worth the state to beat him."[32]

People from other sections of the state were jubilant, too. The editor of the Athens *Southern Banner* could find no words to express his gratification that the "scalawag" candidates for the "office of the United States Senator... [had] been de-feated...."[33] From Dalton came a letter to the editor of an Atlanta paper, recalling that just as Judas Iscariot and Benedict Arnold had paid for their treason, Brown was paying for his.[34]

In addition to the political rebuke he received in the Senate race, Brown was abused personally by the press in general. Carey W. Styles, the editor of the newly founded Atlanta *Constitution*, was extremely hard on Brown. On one occasion he apologized profusely for mentioning his name and predicted that Brown would "cheat the devils with whom" he was in consort.[35] Styles declared that Brown should not complain of social ostracism by the better class, because he had never associated with them.[36]

Potentially, the most serious attack on Brown involved a Mrs. Fanny Martin. Some letters that were dated 1865, which supposedly had passed between Brown and the Martin woman, were published in the *Constitution*. These letters were of a romantic nature; specifically, they dealt with a rendezvous in Macon, Georgia and with an illegitimate child, who had died. There were intimations that the outraged husband knew all the details. The letters were obtained by the *Constitution* from an anonymous person in Mississippi, who hoped "they might be of some help to the Democratic party of Georgia."[37]

To clear himself, Brown asked that the letters be turned over to and investigated by a committee of a dozen or more prominent jurists and ministers. A group, including Rev. W. T. Brantly, Judge John Erskine, Judge J. I. Whitaker, and others who were well-acquainted with Brown, did examine the letters and decided that beyond question the letters were forgeries.[38] Even before this report was published, few people had taken the incident seriously.

After having attacked Brown all summer, editor Styles announced, on September 16, 1868, that until "some new occasion arises, our columns will be closed to communications in reference to Joseph E. Brown." (He had been "ventilated" sufficiently to satisfy all people, and should now be allowed to rest.) Styles closed his article with this thrust: "The digger of his own grave, let it be undisturbed, save by the winds and rains of heaven."[39] Thereafter, for well over a year, Styles seldom mentioned Brown.

During the years 1867–68, Brown must have carefully studied the future of the Republican party in Georgia. It is interesting to note that he started a slow movement back to the Democratic party. But during this time he made the most of his political influence in obtaining control of Georgia's Western & Atlantic Railroad by lease and in purchasing stock in the Texas & Pacific Railroad.

CHAPTER 7

The Legal Profession and the Courts

Brown's vocational and educational training was in law. His training was thorough, and his early law practice was a success. He had served as a superior court judge before he became governor. When he resigned as governor in 1865, he returned to the practice of law in Atlanta.

In addition to his preparation and experience during Reconstruction, he had acquired great influence. These things combined to make him one of the best-known lawyers in the state. Consequently, he took part in many of the most important law suits in the state, including the Test Oath case. Following this trial, and shortly after his trip to Washington, he was admitted to practice before the United States Supreme Court.[1] The two most important milestones in Brown's legal career came in the year 1868: first he took part in the Ashburn case; and second, in August, he was appointed chief justice of the state supreme court.

Brown gained a great deal of notoriety in connection with his part in the trial of the "Columbus prisoners." These prisoners were charged with the murder of an obnoxious "scalawag," George W. Ashburn,[2] who was killed by a masked group of men on the night of March 28, 1868, in Columbus, Georgia. Since Georgia, at the time, was under military Reconstruction, General U. S. Grant, then chief of staff of the United States Army, ordered that the "murder of Mr. Ashburn be investigated and justice meted out by Military Commission if the civil courts cannot be relied on."[3]

Subsequently, Brown was retained by the prosecution; he was the only civilian to serve as their legal counsel. The Columbus group had attempted to retain Brown, but he had already been employed by the military authorities. Brown was retained early in June, but his fee was not mentioned until the latter part of the month. General George G. Meade, commanding the Third Army District including Georgia, Florida, and Alabama, who had written General John M. Schofield, secretary of war, concerning Brown's fee, said he had employed Brown because of his legal ability and his "influence and position in the State." After Brown had worked on the case for several days, Meade asked him about the amount of money he expected for his services. According to Meade, Brown replied: "Five thousand dollars." Meade reported that he could not authorize the payment of that amount without the consent of his superiors. Brown convinced Meade that he could get three or four times as much from the other side if he chose, but he added that if his fee was set too high, he would withdraw from the case and disclose no information to the defense. Meade felt that under the circumstances Brown should be retained at that fee,[4] and Schofield approved Meade's decision.[5]

As to the "Columbus Prisoners," some twenty-three men had been arrested for the murder of Ashburn. Many of them were subjected to cruel treatment, such as small cells.[6] The sympathy of many people of the state was with the prisoners to such an extent that contributions were taken up for their defense,[7] although the majority of the prisoners were financially well-off. Because their own means were supplemented by contributions, they were able to hire a brilliant group of lawyers for their defense. Alexander H. Stephens, their chief counsel, was assisted by L. J. Gartrell, Martin J. Crawford, General Henry L. Benning, R. J. Moses, and others.[8]

Before the jury was impaneled, it was rumored that Brown was to get a fee of $10,000 as prosecuting attorney.[9] He was charged with being "ungentlemanly" and "insolent" to women witnesses. On the other hand, the head of the prosecution,

General William M. Dunn, was "complimented for his conduct."[10] The editor of the Selma, Alabama, *Times* stated that
he had a "thousand times" rather be one of the prisoners than
Joe Brown.[11]

In the course of the trial it developed that some of the witnesses
had been paid by the prosecution to testify and that others were
forced to do so. One of the accused, William Duke, it was proven,
was in Meriwether County at the time of the slaying, but a cousin
of his by the same name had been involved in Ashburn's murder.
The arresting officers, who apparently secured the names of
the accused men from informers, arrested the wrong Duke and
never knew the difference. Moreover, some of the prosecution
witnesses' stories contained serious contradictions.[12]

After Rufus Bullock was inaugurated as governor of Georgia
on July 21, and civil government was resumed, Meade ordered
the case suspended. He had asked Grant what position he should
take if Georgia regained its civil status before the trial was complete; but, at the same time, Meade made out a strong case
for a continued military trial, regardless of any change in the
state's position.[13] Nevertheless, the military trial was suspended
on July 23, and the prisoners were released after each one of
them had posted a bond of $2,000. The Atlanta *Constitution*
commented that though both sides were lucky to have the trial
end, it might have been interesting to see what the outcome
would have been; but the trial was never resumed.[14]

Despite all the harsh criticism heaped upon Brown for his
part in the "Columbus Trial," he made no attempt to explain
his position or to defend himself at the time. Eleven years later,
after General Meade's death and shortly before Brown entered
actively into politics again, the ex-governor *did* explain his conduct. His explanation came in 1879 in connection with a legislative investigation of alleged corruption in the executive branch
of the Georgia government. The Georgia Department of the
Treasury was under heavy suspicion. Louis F. Garrard, a state
representative from Muscogee County and a member of the
investigating committee, took the opportunity to make a verbal
attack on Brown after Brown had testified. In the course of
his attack, Garrard referred frequently to the "Columbus pris-

oners" and Brown's part in this trial—a trial that had no connection with the investigation.[15] In answer to the attack, Brown wrote a letter to the Atlanta *Constitution* on September 24, 1879, in which he claimed that public policy in 1868 had kept him from explaining his part in the Ashburn case. He maintained that he knew nothing of the arrest and confinement of the prisoners until General Meade sent for him and asked him to help prosecute the accused men in a military court. Brown said that he pleaded with Meade to wait until the legislature had met and had complied with the Reconstruction acts so that the case could be tried in the civil courts. Meade replied that this was a very serious case and must be prosecuted. He further said that if Brown would not take the case, he knew others who would, and he named the lawyers he had in mind. Brown contended that all of them were rabid Radicals who would have prosecuted the accused men to the full extent of the law. He explained that he had taken the case under these circumstances, but he had taken it with the understanding that if the death penalty was imposed, Meade would delay execution of the sentence until a civil government had been established and given a chance to review the case. Meade's reply to this was to emphasize that the trial was more important than conviction. At the time, Brown had told this story to General William Phillips, a friend of the prisoners, who advised him to take the case with that understanding.[16]

In a second letter, written the next day, Brown attacked Garrard for having criticized his conduct in the Columbus trial, since the trial was not relevant to the present investigation. To make matters worse, Garrard, Brown said, conducted the investigation without allowing him to testify or cross-examine the only witness, who was Garrard himself.[17]

Garrard, meanwhile, had written an answer to Brown's first letter in which he compared Brown to Judas Iscariot and Benedict Arnold. Who could know the truth concerning the agreement between Brown and Meade, Garrard demanded? Meade was dead and Brown was not a fair witness. He scoffed at Brown's argument that he took the case to keep the rabid Radical lawyers from prosecuting it. In 1868, who was more

Radical than Brown?[18] In another letter to the *Constitution*, Garrard charged that Brown had insulted the committee investigating the executive department and that he had written an insulting anonymous letter to the papers about the case. Garrard concluded his letter with some rather personal, derogatory remarks about Brown.[19]

Brown replied that Garrard was receiving information from Brown's enemies outside the legislature. In explaining his Reconstruction policy, he said that he had done in 1868 what most other Southerners did in 1872, because Reconstruction and the amendments were inevitable. In his letter, Garrard had quoted liberally from the 1868 issues of the Atlanta *Constitution*. Brown pointed out that in those days the *Constitution* printed and endorsed anything anti-Reconstruction.[20] He noted, too, that during the same period he had acted as counsel for the defense in other military trials and had won the cases.[21]

After the Brown–Garrard controversy had been well-publicized, Brown began to gather witnesses. Carey W. Styles, the editor and founder of the *Constitution*, announced that he was sorry he had criticized Brown so harshly in 1868. The situation had changed, he said, and Brown was not a bad man after all.[22] Major Campbell Wallace, a respected Atlanta banker, wrote that while he was superintendent of the Western & Atlantic Railroad in 1868, General Meade had told him the same story about the Ashburn case that Brown had recently made public.[23] John B. Peck of Charleston, South Carolina, who had been an intimate friend of Meade, recalled that in 1868 the General was impatient for the legislature to convene so that he could suspend the trial.[24]

Alexander H. Stephens, however, was Brown's most influential witness. He confirmed the story that Brown had told of his agreement with the military authorities. He further stated that Brown had suggested that Stephens, as chief defense counsel, might separate the cases and try them one at a time so as to avoid the conviction by implication of some of the defendants who definitely were not guilty. Moreover, this method would have the additional advantage of prolonging the case by trying one person at a time. Stephens refused to consent to this plan because he knew he had enough evidence to free all of the prisoners; for he had witnesses to prove that the men who were guilty of the murder had planned to "tar and feather" Ashburn, but that when they went to get him, he fired on them, and they shot him in self-defense.[25]

In addition to Garrard, there were others who criticized Brown and his part in the Ashburn case, as well as his 1879 explanation of it. A North Georgia paper remarked that "when ex-Governor Brown says he took a fee of $5,000 from the United States authorities to prosecute the 'Columbus prisoners' while he was determined to do all in his power to acquit them, he makes a confession that would destroy the reputation of any lawyer."[26]

On the other hand, the editor of the Atlanta *Constitution* said that he was glad that the case had been brought up again because it cleared up so many things and absolved so many of the men involved in it. He now had more respect for all of them—for Brown, for Stephens, and especially for General Meade.[27] Brown was pleased that the case had been revived. In writing to his friend L. N. Trammell about the controversy, he declared that in that "regard my enemies did me a kindness by giving me an opportunity"[28] to explain.

If Brown's story of the agreement with Meade was completely true, the general was either a good actor or Brown had talked him into the agreement after Meade had failed to persuade Schofield and Grant to continue the military trial in the event that Georgia formed a civil government.[29] In 1868, one immediate result of the Ashburn case was Brown's defeat in the Senate race. The election was held in the same month that the trial took place, and Brown's defeat was partially due to his participation in it. In 1879, the case was reopened, and Brown's explanation of his part in it prepared the people for the news of his return to active politics in 1880.

Although he had been beaten in the Senate race in 1868, Brown had helped elect Bullock as governor. Shortly afterward, Brown was appointed chief justice of the Georgia supreme court. Many people believed that he had received the judicial post as a reward for his help to the party and as a consolation for his defeat.

The first reports of his appointment were that he and H. K. McKay would be made associate justices while Chief Justice Hiram Warner would remain in that position.[30] Though Warner had been born in Massachusetts, he was not a Republican. However, he had been on the bench since the supreme court's formation in 1845. McKay was a lawyer, but he had no record as a judge; he was rewarded with the appointment because of his work at the constitutional convention in 1867–68.[31]

On August 13, 1868, it was reported that the Georgia senate, in secret executive session, had confirmed Brown's appointment as chief justice and that of Warner and McKay as associate justices. At that time, an Atlanta editor said that the Republicans were merely adding insult to injury in forcing Brown on the people of Georgia, and he lamented the treachery and ingratitude shown Judge Warner and observed that it might be a good thing to abolish the supreme court.[32] Nevertheless, the appointment was made and signed on August 14.[33]

A number of people in Columbus, Georgia were especially outraged by Brown's appointment. An editor there said the Georgia senate had disgraced itself in allowing Brown to "wear the mantle that once rested upon the head of Joseph Henry Lumpkin" after the people of Georgia had decided in the Senate race that he was not a proper colleague even for Wade and Sumner.[34] Meanwhile, R. J. Moses, a Columbus lawyer, published a letter to the Georgia Bar Association advocating that cases be submitted to arbitration and settled in that manner rather than to submit them to a court presided over by Brown.[35]

In the weeks that followed his appointment, members of the Atlanta bar asked Warner not to resign his post because of his demotion. Warner gave them his assurance that he would remain on the bench.[36] As was expected, his subsequent decisions revealed that he was the conservative member of the court.

By far the most important case decided by the court over which Brown now presided was one involving the eligibility of Negroes to hold office. Before he became chief justice, Brown spoke at Marietta, Georgia, advocating the new state constitution, which, he explained did not give the freedmen the privilege of holding office. Neither the United States Constitution nor

Congress had yet conferred that right, so it followed that the freedmen were ineligible to hold office. The right to hold office, Brown said, was a birthright of the white people.[37]

It must be remembered that this speech was a political one, designed to win votes for the new constitution, not a legal argument. As a judge, he looked at the question under a different light. In the elections under the new state constitution, which was approved in 1868, twenty-nine Negroes were elected to the general assembly. They were seated in July 1868, but in September they were expelled by the members of that body on the grounds that the right to vote did not confer the right to hold office.[38] While Bullock pleaded with Congress to intercede in Georgia and send the army to reinstate the expelled members, a test case on the question was prepared for the courts.

The case came up from Chatham County. In the January term of court in the Eastern Superior Circuit at Savannah, the White vs. Clements case was heard. Richard W. White, a Negro, and William J. Clements, a white man, had been the only two candidates for the office of clerk of the superior court. White won the election, but the results were contested by Clements on the grounds that a person of color could not hold office. A jury ruled that White was one-eighth Negro and therefore ineligible.[39]

Subsequently, the case came before the state supreme court. On June 15, 1869, the court rendered its opinion and decided that the Negro, Richard White, was eligible to hold the office. Brown and McKay concurred in the decision, while Warner dissented. In writing the majority opinion, Brown held that:

> Whatever may or may not be the privileges and immunities guaranteed to the colored race, by the Constitution of the United States and of this State, it cannot be questioned that both Constitutions make them citizens. And I think it very clear that the Code of Georgia upon which alone I base this opinion, which is binding upon all her inhabitants while of force, confers upon all her citizens the right to hold office, unless they are prohibited by some provision found in the Code itself. I find no prohibition in the Code affecting the rights of this respondent.[40]

In essence, Brown ruled, while the Constitution did not grant White the right to hold office, neither did it nor the code of Georgia deny him that privilege.

On the other hand, Judge Warner, in his dissenting opinion said "that there was no existing law of this State which confers the right upon the colored citizens thereof to hold office therein, and consequently that the Defendant has no legal right to hold or exercise the duties of office. . . ."[41] Most of the editorial comments on the decision were unfavorable to Brown. The editor of an Augusta paper said, "It was to be expected that one so profound and adept in the art of dissimulation, and so reckless of principle and consistency, would find little difficulty in giving reasons for his treachery which would be quite satisfactory to himself and those whom he now so abjectly serves."[42] A Savannah editor was "mortified and disgusted" with the decision and blamed the "Radical Junta at Washington" for it.[43]

In his decision, Brown had the support of Alexander H. Stephens. In a published letter to General A. R. Wright, Stephens wrote that he believed the decision was in accordance with the "law and Constitution." If he had been on the bench, Stephens said, he would have come to the same conclusion.[44]

Although the case of the eligibility of Negroes to hold office was decided, the main question, that of the expelled Negro legislators, was yet to be settled. Stephens expressed the view that the general assembly was the sole judge, constitutionally, of the qualifications of its own members. The federal courts, he said, had no jurisdiction over the matter; consequently, no avenue of appeal was open.[45] Even so, the Negroes still had not been reseated in December 1868, when Bullock succeeded in getting Congress to pass a Reconstruction Act for Georgia. General Alfred H. Terry was sent there as a military dictator to purge the legislature and reseat the expelled members elected earlier in the year.[46] The decision of the Georgia Supreme Court, however, remained uncontested, and the state had Negro legislators until the early years of the twentieth century.

After Brown had served for about fourteen months on the Supreme Court, he resigned as chief justice, but he was reappointed by Bullock. This procedure was a political trick by Bullock to purge Warner from the court. An increase in pay was voted for supreme court justices, but in order to qualify for the raise, the justices had to resign and be reappointed because the constitution prohibited officials from receiving increments voted to themselves during their term of office. Brown qualified for the increase. Warner knew that if he resigned he would not be reappointed, so he continued to receive the same salary.[47]

In December 1870, Brown joined a company to bid for the lease of the Western & Atlantic Railroad. To avoid conflict of interest, he wrote Bullock on December 24 that he irrevocably tendered his resignation.[48] It was obvious that he would rather become one of the state's foremost industrialists than to remain a member of the state's highest court.

CHAPTER 8

FROM RADICALISM TO LIBERALISM

While Brown was serving as chief justice during 1869 and a part of 1870, he did not openly participate in politics. He did, however, write personal letters to Alexander Stephens asking him to support John Erskine for membership on the United States Supreme Court[1] and attempting to convince Stephens that Georgia should ratify the Fifteenth Amendment.[2]

As a result of Georgia's refusal to ratify the Fifteenth Amendment, to reseat the Negro legislators, and to outlaw the Ku Klux Klan, the state was subjected to a third Reconstruction late in 1869. Nelson Tift, a congressman from Albany, Georgia who opposed the new Reconstruction, attempted to secure evidence that the activities of the Klan were not as widespread or as outrageous as Governor Bullock had claimed. Brown was among the Georgians whom Tift asked to give testimony in support of his contention. In his statement, Brown admitted that, in certain parts of the state where there had been lawlessness and violence, both Negroes and white Republicans had been victims of the Ku Klux.

But after the elections in November, the excitement over the activities of the Klan subsided and peace and order prevailed for a time. Thereafter, the native white Republicans opposed further Congressional Reconstruction. It has been stated that this incident was the beginning of Brown's break with Bullock.[3]

Tift's survey was followed closely by a letter of inquiry from

70

I. W. Avery, editor of the Atlanta *Constitution*. He asked Brown's opinion on the legality of the second military Reconstruction of Georgia and on what Georgia legislators should do under the circumstances. Because of his position "on the Supreme Court bench," Brown refused to answer the first question, but he did not think it improper to answer the second.

He pointed out that had Southerners acquiesced before, Reconstruction would have been much easier; since the North was the conqueror, it could force its will on the South. But popular oratory, he said, had turned the people's minds toward inaction and people "who foresaw and foretold the calamities which would follow were denounced as traitors. . . ."[4]

As to what to do in the crisis, Brown said it was his "decided conviction that every patriotic member of the Legislature, no matter by what party name he may be known, who can conscientiously take either of the oaths prescribed by the Acts of Congress should attend promptly in obedience to the call of the Governor and qualify without hesitation. Surely we have had enough of the *non-action* policy." He declared that the general financial policy adopted by the state was much more important than "any private or personal ambition."[5]

Brown criticized the management of the state-owned Western & Atlantic Railroad. The people had "a right to require that . . . [it] be managed with ability and economy. . . ." The road in the past, he recalled, had paid money into the treasury and "it is right to expect and demand that . . . [it] shall not be diminished in the future." To correct the mismanagement of the road, he advised that every member of the legislature "be in his place." "The public debt must be paid and the public credit must be maintained at the highest point."[6]

But aside from financial matters, Brown said, "The interest of the state imperatively demands that our relations with the national government shall be reestablished and peace and harmony restored; and that the state shall again be represented in Congress with as little delay as possible." This was necessary, he said, to protect property and decrease crime and lawlessness. "These results," he said, "can never be attained by non-action or resistance to the reconstruction policies of Congress. . . ."[7]

To restore Georgia's position in Congress, Brown believed that the people must reorganize the legislature as Congress directed and adopt the Fifteenth Amendment. "That will now settle the question," said Brown. "Nothing short of it will." Why should the people of Georgia oppose the Fifteenth Amendment, he reasoned, when Negro suffrage was already firmly entrenched in the state? Negro suffrage in the South was required by the Reconstruction acts. But Ohio had not been reconstructed so Negroes there were not allowed to vote. Brown wrote that the "Legislature should not hesitate, under the circumstances, to vote to make the practice uniform in all the States, North or South."[8]

Newspaper comment was not so critical of Brown's letter as it had been of some of his letters in the past. The editor of a Milledgeville paper said that acceptance of the Fifteenth Amendment "would be paying too high a price for the privilege of being represented in Congress." On the other hand, he agreed with Brown's position on the management of the Western & Atlantic Railroad and said, "No man in the State knows better than he what the State Road, under proper management, can do." Brown, he concluded, was the leader of a "reserve corps" and could save the state from plunder, if he would.[9]

Even so, editor I. W. Avery of the Atlanta *Constitution* was certain that Brown, in his reply, would attempt to review his Reconstruction policy of acquiescence. "It was particularly desirable," said Avery, "that the views of all leading men believed to be opposed to Bullock's extreme measures should be obtained."[10]

The communications to Tift and Avery from Brown were proof that he was breaking with Bullock and his Radicals. Although the legislature had been purged by General A. H. Terry and the reorganized body had passed the Fifteenth Amendment in the purge, deposed Negro legislators were reinstated. Governor Bullock, with all his patronage, was not certain of the tenure of his office. Bullock's term was to expire in 1872, but the legislative terms ended in 1870. Since Bullock knew that the moderate Republicans and Democrats would then control that body, which would probably attempt to impeach him, he attempted to persuade Congress to prolong the military occupation of Georgia and to suspend the state elections.

Meanwhile, just as Bullock had foreseen, the conservatives were hard at work in an attempt to impeach him. Robert Toombs joined them and wrote his friend Alexander Stephens about his trip to "Atlanta to see if . . . [he] could be of any service in the present *coup d'état* of Bullock and his conspirators." Toombs related that the conservatives were uniting on J. E. Bryant, a moderate Republican, as their candidate for speaker of the house and that he "and Joe Brown . . . [were] trying to elect him!" It was a strange association, admitted Toombs, but "you know my rule is to use the devil if I can do better to serve the Country."[11]

Finally on October 31, 1871, when Bullock saw that his impeachment was imminent, he resigned and left the state. He said he was resigning the governorship because he was moving to another state. When the legislature met in November, Benjamin Conley, president of the senate, was inaugurated acting governor[12] and served until January 12, 1872.

An Athens editor, elated over the events, gave Brown credit for the turn in Georgia politics. While he was not always in accord with Brown on public issues, he wrote that it was his "opinion that ex-Governor Brown . . . [was] entitled to great credit for his activity in bringing about a quiet and peaceful solution of the difficulty which, at one time, was threatened."[13]

During the time that Conley served as acting governor, a gubernatorial election was held. In December, James M. Smith, a Columbus Democrat, was unopposed by the Republicans in his campaign to succeed Bullock. Smith's inauguration as governor of Georgia the following January pleased most people in the state; anyone but Bullock, apparently, was satisfactory. Linton Stephens was not so pleased with the prospects of Smith's administration. He predicted that it would be run by a "set of damned cowardly, office-seeking, blundering scoundrels; and it is wholly immaterial whether they are called Radicals or Democrats."[14]

Brown's next political activity was in connection with the national election of 1872. A liberal wing of the Republican party severed itself from the old party and called a convention to meet the following spring in Cincinnati. The convention nominated Horace Greeley for president and B. Gratz Brown for vice president. Although Joseph E. Brown was not a delegate to the convention, he publicly approved its actions.[15] Shortly after the convention, the Democrats met in Baltimore and endorsed the candidates nominated by the Liberal Republicans to oppose President Grant.

In July, the Democrats and the Liberal Republicans held simultaneous state conventions in Georgia. The first order of business, after the organization of the Liberal Republican convention, was a motion made by Brown to appoint a committee to suggest to the Democratic convention that the two parties merge. The motion was carried. Brown was appointed chairman of the group to prepare the communication and to write a comprehensive letter.[16]

On receiving the communication, the Democratic convention appointed a committee to confer with the Liberal Republican committee. After some difficulty as to which party would appear on the electoral ticket, they decided that the Democrats should have that privilege. It was further agreed that the Liberal Republicans would not be obligated to support the Democratic candidates for state offices.[17]

As the general election neared, John L. Hull, a Liberal Republican from Thomaston, Georgia, asked Brown what the policy of the party should be with regard to the approaching election. In reply, Brown recapitulated the events at the state party conventions that involved the party name on the electoral ticket. Brown contended that party names were not as important as the principles involved.[18]

Brown described the Democratic party as one that, in the South, had spent five years of unprofitable, and even costly, opposition to Reconstruction. Now, he declared, it had accepted the three reconstruction amendments. He said that since "this action . . . [had] been wisely taken by the Democratic party, the only difference which . . . [existed] between it and the Liberal Republican party . . . [was] a difference of name." Brown was unable to see why the two groups should not cooperate and "support the same national and state ticket."[19]

Brown wrote Hull that the Liberal Republicans should support Smith in the state election. After all, the Democrats were supporting the Liberal candidate for president, and Governor Smith had "integrity, ability and capacity. . . ." "As he is the nominee of the party who supports Greeley and [B. Gratz] Brown," he said, "and in his letter of acceptance pledges himself individually to their support . . . it seems to me to be the natural course for all who desire the election of Greeley and Brown to cast their suffrage for Governor Smith."[20]

The Atlanta *Constitution* did not comment editorially on Brown's letter, but published a statement—a glowing tribute to Brown—from the Columbus *Sun*, which had been highly critical of Brown on the Ashburn trial. The statement compared him to a missionary and a Quaker as well as to an Indian fighter. His oratory, it said, had "none of the furious unchained whirlwind eloquence of Toombs, the sophistry, vanity and savage denunciation, and invective of Hill," but was "more natural and practical than the latter two combined."[21]

Concurrent with the political merging of the Liberal Republicans and Democrats in Georgia, Brown became involved in a serious dispute with Toombs, which almost led to a duel. The difficulty arose over property that had been deeded by Samuel Mitchell to the state for the purpose of building a railroad terminal when the Western & Atlantic Railroad was in its infancy. Over the years since 1842, when it was donated, the plans for the depot were changed, and the land was involved in several exchanges. By 1867, it was the site of a city park in the heart of Atlanta. In that year, Brown, as counsel, brought suit for the heirs of Mitchell for the land on the grounds that it had been given for a railroad terminal, but it had not been used for that purpose. Subsequently, a measure was introduced in the general assembly to resolve the dispute with the Mitchell heirs.[22]

Meanwhile, Brown became chief justice of the supreme court of Georgia and gave the case to his law partner, O. A. Lochrane. In 1870, a compromise was completed and accepted by the heirs and by the general assembly. Part of the agreement was that the heirs were to pay the state $35,000 in lieu of the taxes that would have been assessed since 1842. Before the compromise, the general assembly was offered $100,000 for the state's claim by Alfred Austell. Shortly after the agreement was made, the heirs sold part of the newly-acquired property to Ezekial Waitzfelder of New York and his business partner, Joseph E. Brown, for $50,000.00.[23]

In June 1872, Robert Toombs wrote a letter to the Griffin *Daily News* about the case. He charged that the general assembly, which had been purged by General A. H. Terry, had passed the bill by pressure and bribery on the part of Brown, Lochrane, and H. I. Kimball. Toombs said Brown "engineered" the bill through the legislature in the name of the "orphans of Mitchell."[24]

Brown answered Toombs on July 3, 1872 in one sentence: "Now if General Toombs intends by this language to say that I have been guilty of bribery in 'engineering' this bill through the Legislature, I pronounce his statement an infamous falsehood and its author an unscrupulous liar."[25]

After another letter from Toombs on July 11, containing more charges,[26] Brown revealed that a duel had been proposed. He said John C. Nichols, a friend of Toombs, came into his office and asked to speak to him privately. Brown quoted Nichols as saying: "On account of your church relations, General Toombs does not know whether you hold yourself amenable to the code, and while I admit this is an irregular proceeding in behalf of General Toombs, I make the inquiry." Brown replied that General Toombs had "nothing to do with ... [his] church relations." "If he desires to send me a communication," he said, "I am ready to receive it at any moment." Brown said that after the conversation with Nichols, he wrote an account of it and sent it to Toombs, who meanwhile had left Atlanta on the day of the conversation. Toombs never delivered the challenge.[27]

A Washington, D. C. newspaper commented that "Toombs' refusal to fight was quite as much a matter of surprise to Georgia as Brown's readiness to do so."[28] Most people, including Toombs, apparently thought that Brown would refuse a challenge because he was a deacon in the Baptist church. But Brown prepared to resign that office and did some work on a will in preparation for the duel.[29] It is significant, too, that the editor of the Augusta *Chronicle and Sentinel,* a paper that strongly backed Toombs, never mentioned the incident.[30]

The proposed duel had its reflections at the state university, where in the same year, one student challenged another to a duel. David C. Barrow agreed to act as a second in the duel, and for that reason was suspended from school by the faculty. David's brother, Benjamin, wrote his father about his brother's troubles and lamented that "Bob Toombs and Joe Brown, two Trustees . . . [had] caused all these recent duels in Georgia. They ought to be expelled from the board of trustees before any student is punished for duelling." Benjamin thought that Brown had disgraced himself and that "the Baptist Church . . . [had] made itself ridiculous by its subservience to him."[31]

More important for Brown, said a contemporary biographer of Toombs, was the fact that "General Toombs gave him the opportunity to appear in a better light than he had appeared for a long time; this incident was the beginning of his return to popularity and influence in Georgia."[32]

Brown began to gain more influence after the Toombs difficulty and the political merger in 1872. Now his opinions were being sought for publication on important public issues. One such instance came in 1873 when the general assembly was in the process of repudiating questionable bonds issued by the Bullock administration. The editor of the Atlanta *Constitution* and thirty members of the general assembly asked for Brown's views on the subject. He replied in a voluminous letter that covered a whole page of the newspaper. He declared that repudiation of the state bonds would not be upheld by the courts and that the general assembly indicated fear of this fact when they refused to compromise or be sued under the protection of the Eleventh Amendment to the United States Constitution. He further believed that it would cost Georgia more in the long run to repudiate the bonds than to honor them. Repudiation would render future state bonds almost worthless on the market, and even if they could be sold, the interest on them would be extremely high. Thus, he said, repudiation would bring unbearable taxes.[33]

Brown's opinion of the civil rights bill then pending in Congress in 1874 was probably most timely and influential in aiding his return to the Democratic party. He contended that the South gave assent to all the measures required of them in Reconstruction and had been readmitted to the Union, therefore, Reconstruction measures should cease. The states, he said, were at last capable of governing themselves. Nevertheless, the Southern whites were not blameless in the civil rights problem, because they could have controlled the Negro vote. Instead, they declared themselves hostile to that course early in Reconstruction. Consequently, because their former masters would not advise them, the Negroes turned to the "carpetbaggers," who were quite willing to use them in politics.[34]

This civil rights bill dealt with the mixing of the races on trains, in hotels, and in other public places, which led Brown to say it was a "social rights measure" rather than a civil rights bill. He maintained that the purpose of it was to force "social equality between the white and colored people of the South." "This can never be done," he said, "and if attempted, should not and will not be submitted to, be the consequences what they may. God has created the two races different, with different tastes, capacity and instincts for social enjoyment, and no human legislation can ever compel them to unite as social equals."[35]

The consequences of the enforcement of such an act would be a disaster, he believed. "The legislature of each southern state, as soon as it is called together, will at once repeal all laws by which the public schools are maintained at the public expense, and leave each man to educate his own children as best he can. This will leave the colored people who are without property to grope their way in ignorance with no means of educating their offspring, and it will necessarily leave a great many white people in the same unfortunate position." "But," he continued, "be this as it may, we will never submit to mixed schools where our children shall be compelled to unite with those of the colored race, upon terms of social equality." "It cannot be said that we violate any provision of the constitution of the United States, when we repeal our school laws, as that constitution requires no state to maintain any public school. . . ."[36]

But Brown feared that even worse results might come from attempts to enforce the acts. Compulsory mixing would lead to "constant strife, and very frequent bloodshed." He thought that general anarchy and ultimately the "extermination of the Negro race" would follow and that any attempts to use the army to enforce such acts would fail unless Negro troops were used.[37]

While most people in Georgia agreed with Brown's views on civil rights, there were some who did not trust his motives. Some letters that were severely critical of him appeared in papers over the state. But Carey Styles, an editor of an Albany paper, and formerly one of Brown's harshest critics as an Atlanta editor, now came to his defense. Styles thought he knew the names of two of the anonymous letter writers and commented that they were "unfit to unlatch Governor Brown's carriage driver's shoe buckle...."[38] An Atlanta *Constitution* editor stated that Brown's services to the Democratic party should be accepted and turned to the best advantage. He, too, deprecated the "constant flings" at Brown.[39]

Thus Brown was about to complete the circuit of the political parties. He had been a Democrat in 1860, a Confederate in 1861, a Johnson and Union man in 1865, a Republican in 1867, a Liberal Republican five years later; and now, in 1874, he was knocking on the door for readmission to the Democratic party. All he needed to become a full-fledged member was the chance to do some outstanding service for the party. That chance came in 1876.

CHAPTER 9

Rejoins the Democrats

Brown found the chance he needed to make himself an honored member of the Democratic party again in the election of 1876. In the fall of that year, hoping to get rid of a throat irritation, he traveled out to Colorado, back across the Northern states, and thence to Georgia. The trip gave him a chance to observe the political affairs of these states. Since Brown was "universally conceded in all this section" to have more political judgment "than any livng man," he was interviewed on the prospects of the outcome of the approaching presidential election.[1]

The choice between Samuel J. Tilden, Democrat, and Rutherford B. Hayes, Republican, Brown believed, would be very close, "with the chances decidedly favoring Tilden." Tilden had the advantage, he said, because of the military action Grant had taken in South Carolina. Many Northern Republicans feared that a military dictatorship might also be imposed upon their own states. Brown said, too, that he had met many former Republicans who planned to vote Democratic because they simply "wanted to see things changed around." These opinions, he added, were formed after talking to ordinary people over the country.

The election on November 7, 1876 resulted in a dispute over

Part of this chapter is reprinted with permission from *Florida Historical Quarterly.*

the returns in Florida, South Carolina, Louisiana, and Oregon. Success in any one of these states would have brought victory for the Democrats. Florida, it seemed, would be a logical state on which to center attention. While the state officials were Republicans, most of the county officials who had been recently elected were Democrats. This gave the Democrats the power to appoint local election officials. In the November election, the Democrats gave Tilden a majority in the state and elected a Democratic governor, but the results were contested by the Republicans, who charged the Democrats with fraud and illegal voting. Counter-charges by the Democrats followed.[2]

On November 12, Brown received a telegram from Abram S. Hewitt, of New York, chairman of the Democratic executive committee, in which Hewitt said he and the party "earnestly" desired that Brown "go immediately to Florida and see that there is a fair and honest count and return."[3]

There were other requests, including a long petition signed by Atlanta people, asking that he go to Florida. Despite the rather serious throat irritation, which had made the Colorado trip necessary earlier in the year, he agreed to go.[4] His secretary and P.M.B. Young, a north Georgia Democrat went along with him, as well as some thirteen other Democrats, most of whom were from Pennsylvania.[5]

Shortly after the election, Henry W. Grady went to Florida to represent the Atlanta *Constitution* and the New York *Herald*. On November 14, he reported to the *Constitution* that Joe Brown had "arrived and settled down to work."[6] Grady, who a few months before had been writing violently anti-Brown editorials, now wrote about how glad he was to see Brown. Said Grady, "Wellington did not need Blucher more sorely in the crisis of the memorable day at Waterloo, than did the democrats of this state and the nation need Joe Brown when that gentleman quietly walked into the Warwick hotel [in Tallahassee] this morning. I was never so glad to see a man in my life! The democrats are not the men for the crisis."[7]

Grady continued his reports on the situation in Florida. Except for two or three Democrats there, no one had any conception of the political situation, he said. The whole party was "inert and inactive" and the Democratic nominee for governor, George F. Drew, was still at home. The Democratic party had no campaign headquarters, no clerks employed and no organization; further, it had no money for any purpose. Those "who sent dispatches paid the toll themselves." Potentially more detrimental to the Democrats' campaign than their lack of money and enthusiasm was the arrival of W. E. Chandler, who was, according to Grady, "the smartest political adjustor in the north." Chandler had a blank check, with full authority to fill it out, and willing workers to aid him in the Republican cause.[8]

Under these unfavorable circumstances, Brown went to work. Two hours after his arrival, Grady wrote, "he had been all through the Florida law" on elections. After a meeting with local managers, Brown, "with a smile on his lips and business in his eyes," told Grady that "things . . . [were] moving beautifully." The Democrats had acquired the necessary money; they would "make no errors of omission or commission." Even though it was "exceedingly inconvenient," Brown planned to stay in Florida until the dispute was settled.[9]

The Florida muddle moved from bad to worse. The Republican governor of the state, Marcellus Stearns, appointed a board, made up of two Republicans and one Democrat, to canvass the disputed precincts. The Democrats filed an injunction against this action in Leon County, but despite the logical argument by Brown and others, the appointment of the canvassing board was sustained. Brown's argument for the injunction was what Grady called "an exceedingly able opinion." His speech "won the highest plaudits of . . . [the day], and absolutely settled the law of the case."[10] Brown held that the governor of a state had no right to appoint a canvassing board because one was already established by law, composed of the attorney general, the secretary of state, and the comptroller.[11]

Brown remained in Florida to help argue the Democratic cause before the canvassing board. Brown's speech, Grady reported, was "very exciting." He "gave the radical members thereof occasion to remember that he . . . [was] remaining in Florida for his health."[12] Following his speech before this board, Brown reported that Florida was "probably certain" for Tilden.[13] On the day the canvassing board finished its count, it was reported that the telegraph wires from Tallahassee were out of order.[14] Grady drove a rented team of horses to the nearest telegraph facilities at Drifton and in a "scoop" reported that the board had counted a majority of the precincts in favor of Hayes and the Republicans.[15]

Brown commented: "The dark deed of infamy is done by throwing out democratic counties and precincts in the teeth of the evidence and in shameless violation of the law." He said further that the "radical majority of the board of canvassers . . . declared the Hayes electors entitled to certificates." Nevertheless, the attorney general, a Democrat and a member of the board, declared the Democratic electors victorious and issued certificates to them.[16] Thus the Florida situation was not settled—it was up to Congress to decide which slate of electors was valid.

On his return to Atlanta, Grady reported that Brown had been seriously ill during the Florida trouble. Along with his throat ailment, he had suffered from pneumonia, which might have been "fatal in this changeable climate." His bed was surrounded by stacks of law books, which were read to him, and ill as he was, he "made up the skeleton of the legal argument" upon which the Democrats based their case.[17]

En route from Florida to Atlanta by train, Brown was approached by two prominent Republicans from Ohio who asked his opinion of the Florida situation. Members of Brown's party believed that these men were sent to Brown at Hayes's request. Brown told them he was "morally certain" the state had given Tilden a clear majority; the Hayes majority had been built up by direct and simple fraud. "No man who had a regard for the good opinion of his fellow-people could take the presidential chair on such a title as was furnished by Florida."[18]

Back in Atlanta, Brown told a newspaper reporter that nothing could be done to keep the Republicans from taking the Florida vote. He said that the Democrats had collected enough evidence to convince anyone of the fraud, but that the Democrats labored under the disadvantage of having the state government controlled by the Republicans. The Republicans also had the occupying troops to aid them in collecting fraudulent affidavits. Even

Captain Mills, who had played a part of some importance in the Ashburn trial, was disgusted with the work that he and his military unit had had to do for the Republicans.[19]

To his friend, L. N. Trammell, Brown stated that he did not "suppose that any human effort or human foresight could have prevented the result" in Florida. However, he pointed out that there was still a chance that Tilden might win: "We must leave this matter in the hands of our northern democratic friends. If they stand firm and show no disposition to waver, we will inaugurate Tilden without difficulty, in my opinion. But if there is any backing down of the democracy in the north, the military will take the matter in charge and inaugurate Hayes by military force. This will be a subversion of our republican form of government and our future will be that of subjects of a military depotism."[20]

Meanwhile, the Democratic governor of Oregon certified a Democratic elector to cast the disputed vote of that state, which would have given Tilden the votes that he needed to be elected. Although this decision did not settle the election, most Democrats, including those in Atlanta, thought it did. Consequently, on the night of December 12, 1876, a torchlight parade was staged to celebrate Tilden's victory. Charles Fairbanks, an Atlanta artist, made some drawings on posters that were illuminated and carried in the night processional. It included coats of arms of southern states and pictures of a number of prominent people, including Brown. Under Brown's picture was the motto: "My judgment is we are all right." Another poster carried a slogan reading: "A man named Brown/took them down." The parade ended in front of the Markham House, where E. Y. Clarke opened the exercises by reading a letter from Brown.[21]

In this letter Brown explained his inability to appear on the program by saying that he had been stricken with pneumonia in Florida and that his physicians had advised him not to go out into the night air to speak to the gathering. He believed, as other Democrats did, that Tilden would be inaugurated and that the Oregon vote would not be questioned. The Republican Congress would not investigate the Oregon vote because that would create a strong case for the Democrats to investigate the

Republican frauds in Florida, Louisiana, and South Carolina. Under these circumstances, Brown said, "Believing that this will be the result and feeling that it gives us great cause for congratulation and rejoicing, I sincerely unite with you in the joy to which you will give expression on the . . . occasion."[22]

The press of Georgia was proud of Brown's efforts in Florida. An Augusta editor said: "Those who know the importance of Governor Brown's business interests can realize the magnitude of the sacrifice he is making. Governor Brown has labored earnestly and skillfully to prevent the Radicals from stealing the electoral votes of Florida from Mr. Tilden, and he deserves the thanks of the Democrats of Georgia and of the Democracy of the whole country."[23]

An Atlanta editor said that his "labors in Florida in behalf of justice and right have been arduous and long conditioned, and it is probably owing to his efforts, more than to any other cause, that the democrats of that state will be able to make such an overwhelming and infamous showing of fraud on the part of the radicals."[24] On the trip from Florida, Grady wrote it was "quite a noticeable fact that of the crowd who boarded the special train bearing the 'visiting statesmen' home, nine-tenths of them asked for Governor Brown first." Grady proclaimed him "the hero of the campaign and the hero of the homeward march."[25]

In a Rome, Georgia paper, an article on Brown characterized him as "a perfect man, the noblest work of God."[26] Brown, who was quite proud of his work in Florida, too, declared, "I feel the consciousness of having done at my own expense all that it was in my power to do there to protect the right and avert a calamity."[27]

The settlement of the dispute came shortly before the inauguration of the president on March 4, 1877. Congress appointed an electoral commission, and it decided in favor of Hayes, who was inaugurated. Meanwhile, further court action in Florida gave the state government to the Democrats and George F. Drew was sworn in as governor.

The work of the electoral commission was augmented by an agreement that was reached between certain members of both political parties. Included in this group were Senator John B.

Gordon of Georgia and Representative John Young Brown of Kentucky, both of whom were Democrats, and Representative Charles Foster and an attorney, Stanley Mathews, both of whom were Ohio Republicans. Their meetings took place in Mathews' room in the Wormley House in Washington. In these negotiations, the Democrats consented to allow Hayes' inauguration, if, in return, his administration would end Reconstruction in the South, give some offices to Democrats, and help build the Southern Pacific Railroad.[28]

Although the news of the agreement was not made public, Brown found out about it. He was most displeased. Writing under the nom de plume "Citizen," he exposed the agreement. He contended that had the commission been voted down by the House, they might have waited until presidential inauguration day, March 4, 1877, when the election would have been thrown into the Democratic House and Tilden would have been elected. He would then have removed the troops and ended Reconstruction in the South. As it happened, the Democrats gained nothing more than they would have received under any circumstances, and they had lost the presidential election in the bargain.[29]

In discussing the details of the agreement, Brown compared the situation in 1877 to the Adams–Clay "bargain" in 1824 when Henry Clay supported John Quincy Adams in the Congressional election for the presidency. In return, Adams appointed Clay secretary of state. Brown said that if no trade was made between the parties, then there was certainly a "capital understanding." He closed his letter with a statement to the effect that Gordon and John Young Brown had taken too much authority into their own hands and that "the consummation of that capital understanding . . . [was] not a feather in the cap of either of these statesmen."[30]

Gordon supporters were quick to ask for the name of the anonymous writer. Brown instructed the newspaper to publish his statement that he was the "Citizen."[31] In reply to it, Gordon denied any part in a trade. Brown then printed copies of letters between the principals in the agreement. He also answered charges by Gordon's supporters that he was a candidate for a Senate post. Brown replied that he was not a "candidate for election to the United States Senate, to fill the place now filled by General Gordon, at the expiration of his term...."[32]

Brown's Reconstruction record was then attacked by the Gordon forces. To this charge, he replied that he had been a Republican in only one national campaign, the one in 1868. While he had been a Republican, he was consistent and loyal. Nevertheless, said Brown, "I never was a party to the sale of four years of democratic administration for the performance of a single act by the opposition. And I certainly never would assume the responsibility as he [Gordon] did of making a trade for my party, if I could not make a better one than was made by him and his associates."[33]

The Atlanta *Constitution*, by this time a Brown supporter but by no means an enemy of Gordon, had nothing to say, editorially, about the Brown–Gordon controversy. Dr. E. L. Connally, Brown's son-in-law, wrote Brown that E. P. Howell, president of the *Constitution*, told him that papers all over the state were "pitching into him for not having something to say about the Brown–Gordon correspondence...." Connally said that Howell went to see Brown to try to persuade him not to publish his latest letter, but he could not find him. Said Connally, "I told him he would see which was the strong side before it was stopped."[34]

The New Orleans *Democrat* deprecated the dispute in view of all the work Gordon had done as a "visiting statesman" in South Carolina in 1876. Most of all, the editor disliked any hint of a split of any kind in the Democratic party at such a critical time. The real blame for the loss of the presidential election, he said, belonged to Tilden and "his eastern chiefs." "They were too deficient in pluck and common manliness to maintain what was gained," the editor said.[35]

Shortly after the election dispute was settled in 1877, the movement to write a new state constitution resulted in a call for a constitutional convention. A group of Atlanta businessmen took the opportunity in March 1877 to write a letter to the editor of the Atlanta *Constitution*, in which they said that the best men possible should be elected to "construct the fundamental frame work of our state government in the coming convention." This being so, they suggested a slate of six men to represent Fulton County in the convention, and one of them was Brown.[36]

But Brown's name as a delegate to the convention was not on the official ticket when it appeared. Nevertheless, a combination called "Many Democrats," a group of anti-convention men of the Thirty-fifth Senatorial District, announced their choices for delegates to the convention and included Brown as a write-in candidate.[37] One week later these names were withdrawn,[38] but despite this, Brown received forty-three write-in votes in the election.[39]

Obviously, Brown was disappointed at not being a delegate to the constitutional convention of 1877, since he had been quite active in writing the constitutions of 1865 and 1868. His son-in-law, Connally, was disappointed too and wrote Brown that he had been trying "to find out why it was your name was not on the list of delegates to the Convention." "I have no doubt," Connally said, "executive influence is at the bottom."[40] Governor Alfred H. Colquitt, inaugurated on January 12, 1877, apparently was the "executive influence" to which Connally referred.

Following his trip to Florida in 1876, Brown must have realized that he had regained much of his lost popularity. In reference to his political future, though, he wrote his friend Trammell: "I have only to state that I have no desire to hold any political position under either the state or federal government. If I can be of any service to restoring to our people the old form of government as recognized and administered by our fathers, and in inaugurating an administration that will make the military subordinate to the civil, and secure our local self-government, I shall feel that the result amply rewards me for my labor."[41]

Whether or not Brown desired a public office, his name was mentioned for many positions before the elections of 1876 and 1880. He was most frequently suggested as a candidate for governor. A Cartersville man wrote the Atlanta *Constitution* that after looking over the records of prominent men in 1876 in search of a candidate, he believed none was better than Brown, who was "a tried man, possessing exactly the qualifications to meet our present tendencies."[42] Recalling Brown's work in Florida,

a Rome editor said. "He deserves no less a compliment than
to occupy once more the position of Governor...."[43] Again in
1880, a North Georgia paper stated, "Joseph E. Brown would
no doubt make us a good Governor," and asked, "What say
the people and the press?"[44] Another wanted "Old Joe for our
next Governor," and predicted, "old Georgia will rise Phoenix
like from the ashes."[45]

Brown also had supporters who wanted him to run for the
United States Senate. A Marietta man wrote that after surveying
the field of candidates, which included Thomas M. Norwood
(the incumbent), James M. Smith, James Johnson, and B. H.
Hill, he found only one man who met the requirements and
that one was Brown.[46] An Augusta editor warned Senator Norwood that he should pray that Brown would not "aim at the
Senatorial hole in the ground." He reminded Norwood that
"he always comes out of the hole ahead of everybody, you
know."[47] A reader wrote the Atlanta paper that the "democratic
party of Georgia and ... The United States, would feel secure
if Governor Brown were sent to the senate."[48] But there was
some objection to a Senate race by Brown. A LaGrange paper
stated it poetically: "No, no, It's not for Joe."[49]

During this period Brown was mentioned for other positions
in the national picture. In 1875, it was rumored that he might
replace his business friend, Columbus Delano, as secretary of
the interior in the president's cabinet.[50] Then in 1880, he was
mentioned in Georgia as a possible presidential candidate.[51]

Brown's work in the election of 1876 in Florida aided his
new rise in the Democratic party as much as his part in the
Liberal Republican movement in 1872 had helped him get back
into the Democratic party. He must not have been welcomed
by Gordon, as Brown had castigated him for his part in the
electoral "compromise of 1877." Apparently, Colquitt did not
want Brown to be a delegate to the constitutional convention.
Evidently in 1877, Brown was at odds with both Gordon and
Colquitt, who with Brown himself were later to make up the
Georgia "Triumvirate." Much happened between 1876 and 1880
to bring Brown, Gordon, and Colquitt together. Their alliance
might have been explained by the fact that Brown had the money

necessary to finance political campaigns had not Colquitt had plenty of money himself, or it might have been explained by Brown's rising political popularity. But whatever the bond between them was, it could not have been mutual admiration on either a personal or a political plane.

CHAPTER 10

Toward The New South

The Reconstruction Era was another transitional period for Joseph E. Brown. He used his political experience skillfully to build his economic empire. At the same time, he was second to none in philanthropic endeavors in the Georgia of his time. Both of these pursuits helped to pave the way for the former governor to crown his political career with a seat in the United States Senate from 1880 to 1890.

No doubt the most important economic venture that Brown undertook in the Reconstruction Era was his part in the lease of Georgia's state-owned Western & Atlantic Railroad, which operated between Atlanta and Chattanooga. From 1865 until 1870, the Reconstruction government of the state operated the railroad amid much controversy, inefficiency, and corruption. During this period, not only did the railroad deteriorate as a result of neglect and misuse, but also the state began to lose money by its operation. When a notorious scalawag, Foster Blodgett, became superintendent of the Western & Atlantic in 1870, he asked for a half-million dollar appropriation to repair and reconstruct the road. His request led some editors to suggest that the state lease the railroad.[1]

During this time, Brown was chief justice of the Georgia supreme court, and he actually wrote the lease bill that was passed by both houses of the general assembly and signed by Governor Rufus Bullock in October 1870.[2] In December, Governor Bullock announced the formation of a leasing company. The company was headed by Brown. Among its other members were John S. Delano, son of President U. S. Grant's secretary of the interior, Columbus Delano; Simeon Cameron, a Pennsylvania Republican; H. I. Kimball, an Atlanta scalawag; Benjamin H. Hill; and a hesitant Alexander H. Stephens, who later withdrew from the company.

The lease was to run for twenty years at the rate of $25,000 per month.[3] News of its terms immediately brought on a controversy. Other prospective leasing companies claimed that their bids should have been accepted over that of the company headed by Brown. The successful company was accused of everything from undue influence on the carpetbag governor Rufus B. Bullock to "pay offs" to other influential politicians. Some people protested that no company headed by Brown could be a good one; others objected because such men as Cameron and Delano were members of the company.

All of these objections resulted in legislative investigations of the lease in 1872, 1876, and 1880. These investigations left the general feeling that the company had acquired the lease by fraudulent means, and there was some testimony to that effect. But each time, there was not enough evidence to substantiate the testimony. Further, the $25,000 per month rental was paid on time with a great deal of publicity by the company when it was paid. The improvements and profits made by Brown's leasing company were often contrasted with the deterioration and deficits of the railroad's operation by the state during Reconstruction.[4]

The lessees made a number of improvements and changes that increased and ameliorated the service of the Western & Atlantic. In 1886, the road accepted the "standard gauge" between rails of four feet, eight and one-half inches instead of the gauge of five feet that was ordinarily used by Southern railroads. A standard gauge cut the costs of loading and unloading on shipments on two lines with a different gauge. The change took only a few hours, and there was only a minimal interruption in the schedules of the trains.[5] In the same year, sleeping cars and dining cars were added to the Western & Atlantic rolling

stock and put in service on the runs from Atlanta north to Cincinnati, south to Jacksonville, and west to Little Rock.[6]

Another innovation of the times adopted by the road controlled by Brown was "pooling." Pooling was one of the earliest
methods of rate agreements between railroads which reduced
competition. As a matter of fact, this practice really began in
Atlanta, and the Western & Atlantic was a part of it. The public
was officially notified in April 1878 that one man in an Atlanta
office building would quote rates for cotton shipments for all
companies. The "pooling" was restricted to cotton shipments
only, and "no other agent . . . [had] the right to give a bill of
lading. . . ."[7]

The lease of the Western & Atlantic seemed to be quite satisfactory to the people of Georgia in that just prior to the end of
the Brown lease, the road was leased again. This time the
Nashville, Chattanooga, and St. Louis Railroad was the successful
bidder.[8] None of the previous lessees were involved in the bid-
ding in 1890.

Even so, a new problem presented itself for Brown's group,
though the lease had less than a year to run. It involved what
Brown called "betterments"; that is, an amount of money
estimated to be the difference between what the Western & Atlantic was worth in 1870 and in 1890.

In December 1890, the general assembly created a commission
"to consider the claims between the lessees of the Western &
Atlantic Railroad and the state of Georgia. . . ."[9] Four days later,
on December 26, an act was passed extending the charter of
the old Western & Atlantic lessees past the expiration date of
December 27, 1890 and until the "betterments" question was
settled.[10]

The commission, composed of seven influential Georgians
presided over N. J. Hammond,[11] met at intervals between February 10 and May 23, 1891. The lessees submitted a revised
statement of claims for "betterments," from its original claim
of over $1,500,000 to $722,714.15.[12] However, when the commission reported in May 1891, it reduced that figure and awarded
Brown's company a total of a mere $99,644.04.[13]

Brown never pretended to be a professional railroad man.

His greatest success was in the realm of politics, and he used his political prowess to promote his economic enterprises. In some cases, he used one economic venture to further another. For example, he used his railroad and political power to advance his financial interests in Georgia's coal and iron mines.

In 1873, Brown formed a company, in which he owned half of the stock, to develop the coal and iron mines in northwest Georgia. The company was chartered as the Dade Coal Company, and Brown was listed as its president.[14] Within a year, two more companies, Rising Fawn Iron Company and Walker Iron and Coal Company,[15] both of which were presided over by Brown, were chartered to mine coal and iron in Dade, Bartow, and Walker counties.

Georgia coal, it developed, was more useful in industry than it was for home consumption. An Atlanta iron rolling mill was a heavy consumer of Brown's coal and iron. But just as important, the coal was used by the Western & Atlantic Railroad.[16]

Although the grade of coal and iron in Georgia was not high and the amount was not great, Brown was successful with these ventures: firstly, because he bought the property during the Reconstruction when it was cheap; and secondly, because he used convict labor, which cost very little, to operate the mines.[17] Furthermore, he transported his ore and coal over the Western & Atlantic of which he was also president.

Of all his economic enterprises, Brown said that he most enjoyed his farming experience. "There is less to harass the mind," he said, "and yet unlimited food for it." "If a man has an inclination to study and test scientific principles," he told a Dalton, Georgia newspaper reporter, "there can be no better field."[18] In keeping with his interest in agriculture, the ex-governor acquired lands in areas of Georgia and Texas.

He was also considered something of an expert in "New South" agricultural methods. In his speeches, Brown talked about such things as the use of fertilizer, the diversification of crops, and the reduction of cotton acreage. Furthermore, he advocated the cultivation and exportation of watermelons, peaches, and other fruits.[19]

In his later years, Brown sold most of the stock he owned

in railroads, banks, and other enterprises, but he kept his agricultural lands. He was quoted as saying that he never sold any land because Georgia soil would always be a good investment.[20] No doubt, his "New South" agricultural ideas and practices did make farming profitable for him. But it must be remembered that he was also a shrewd investor in other fields of endeavor, and he successfully applied his general business knowledge to his farm interests.

Even though Brown advocated modern farming methods, a firm farm credit system, and the 1876 Grange movement in which he participated, he had no sympathy for the Populist party. The People's, or Populist, party had grown by leaps and bounds, and by 1892, it posed a serious threat as a third party. Brown wrote some friends in Columbus, Georgia that the Populists were splitting the Democratic party and thus placing the black and white Republicans in perpetual control in politics. "In other words," Brown continued, "it is indispensible to the future prosperity and happiness of the white race of the south that we should maintain, as we have done for many years in the past, a solid south, and to remain solid it is necessary that the whole white race vote democratic [sic] together." At the same time, he believed that no injustice should be done the Negro race.[21]

Brown said he realized that certain classes of Southern people felt that their interests and rights had not been protected; consequently, they had formed a new party. The Democrats, though a major party, had not completely controlled all three branches of the government for the last thirty years; consequently, they had had no chance to pass laws protecting Southern farmers and laborers. How then could the people expect a new third party to get the work done? In Brown's opinion, it would take the Populists longer to have such laws passed than it would the Democrats, who already constituted a major party.[22]

A third party, warned Brown, was destined to failure unless it gained enough strength in its first or second attempt to blot out one of the major parties. There was little doubt in his mind that the Democrats and Republicans would remain dominant and that the People's Party would fail after two tries. He said that family quarrels were always bitter, and he expected the new party to show strength in the 1892 elections. In the event of a good race in 1892, Brown predicted that the People's party would be absorbed by one of the major parties. He marred his record as a good political forecaster though by predicting that the Populists would be absorbed by the Republican party. Actually the Populists were "fused" with the Democrats in the unusual election of 1896.[23]

Whenever Brown became involved in an economic venture, he played a leading part in the enterprise, and he carried this capacity for leadership over to other interests. From his early youth, he had been conscious of the value of education, but his own education had not come easily, and he had never attended any of Georgia's institutions of higher learning. However, during the terms he served as Georgia's Governor, he took great pride in what his administration did for education. He was especially interested in Mercer University and in the University of Georgia.

Brown served on the University of Georgia's board of trustees from 1857 to 1889. During the Reconstruction, when his political speeches brought him infamy, he offered to resign from the board, but his resignation was not accepted. In 1867, he was largely responsible for keeping the University of Georgia open after a student made an inflammatory speech at commencement. He interceded with General John B. Pope and other military authorities who threatened to close the institution because of the incident.[24]

Perhaps the most lasting and valuable contribution, if not the most controversial, was Brown's $50,000 donation to the University of Georgia. In 1882, he proposed to establish the Charles McDonald Brown Scholarship Fund in memory of one of his sons, who had died of consumption in 1881. But because of some strings attached to the gift by Brown and the dedicated opposition of Robert Toombs, the Georgia general assembly rejected the proposal. Finally, Brown consented to a plan to give the money to the University without legislative approval in 1883. He simply bought $50,000 worth of maturing state bonds and presented them directly to the University.[25]

But the ex-governor was less successful in his relations with

Mercer University. Neither Brown nor any of his six sons had attended Mercer. His interest in that institution arose because both he and Mercer were connected with the Southern Baptist denomination. In 1870, Brown raised the money and provided the land to move Mercer from Penfield, Georgia to Atlanta. But the Georgia Baptist convention rejected the invitation to move to Atlanta in favor of one to move to Macon.[26]

Two years before his gift to the University of Georgia, Brown had made another large donation. This one, too, came because of his interest in the Baptist denomination. He offered $50,000 to the Southern Baptist Theological Seminary in Louisville, Kentucky to endow a professorship there, on the condition that the Baptists would not reduce their annual contribution to the institution. Some people have contended that this donation kept the seminary from closing its doors.[27]

In addition to his other contributions to education, Brown served as president of the Atlanta Board of Education from 1869 until 1888. He then served as an honorary member of the board until his death in 1894. His greatest service to public schools was to advocate their expansion in an area and a time in which many people objected to them.[28]

Atlanta was one of the first cities in Georgia to develop its public schools, and Brown was involved in many of the controversies that arose in the course of their operation. In 1873, when the Atlanta city council officially criticized the position of the board of education in the matters of placing white teachers in Negro schools and of reading the Bible in the schools, Brown answered the criticism. The Council condemned the transfer of a white woman of German background from the Negro school, where she had taught mathematics, to a white school. "Do the City Council," asked Brown, "pretend to say that any Southern gentleman or lady, no matter what may be their social position, talent, or qualifications, who has consented to teach colored children, is to be regarded as disgraced, and unfit in the future to occupy any position of honor, trust or profit?" Brown continued, "I wish to reiterate distinctly what I have said on former occasions, that I am not, and never have been, an advocate of social equality, between the races, nor have I ever encouraged or consented to mixed schools. On the other hand, I have always insisted that the races have separate schools and I am unable to see how this principle is violated by the transfer of a very worthy teacher, from the colored schools to the white schools."[29] The transfer was enacted without further incident.

Brown next proceeded to explain his position on the Bible in the schools. "Now, the Jews and Catholics are tax payers, just as Baptists and Methodists are," he said, "and the schools are supported in part by their money; and if they cannot conscientiously send their children to a school where they are taught our version of the Bible, is it right that we should tax them to support the schools where we teach our children these doctrines?" While the controversies between the board of education and the city council continued for at least two more years, the actions of the board of education prevailed in school matters.[30]

In the midst of his economic successes and philanthropic gestures, Brown finally rounded out his political career by attaining a seat in the United States Senate. Senator John B. Gordon resigned his seat in May 1880, and Governor Alfred H. Colquitt appointed Brown to serve until the next meeting of the general assembly in November 1880. Gordon became an attorney for the Louisville & Nashville Railroad, and Colquitt announced his candidacy for reelection as governor. With controversy swirling around this interim appointment and with General A. R. Lawton as his opponent, Brown was elected by the legislature in its next session to serve the remainder of Gordon's term. He was reelected, without opposition, to serve a full term in 1884, and he remained in the Senate until 1890.

Really, he made no great contributions in the Senate. He was a Democrat in an era of Republican domination of national politics. However, he made speeches in the Senate on race relations, on the economic potential of the South, on the wisdom of admitting Utah as a state, and on the advisability of monetizing silver. Though he was considered a Georgia Radical during the Reconstruction, in general his Senate speeches coincided with the views of the national Democratic party.

In the Senate, he received some interesting committee assignments. He served as a member of the Senate Committee on

Foreign Relations in a period when our relations with other international powers were not overwhelmingly successful. Also, he served on the Committee on Labor at a time when labor unions were just developing. But by the time Brown had enough seniority to be influential, his health failed, and he missed some important sessions of the Congress.[31]

From the unfavorable notoriety Brown gained during Reconstruction, it would have been logical to conclude that his political career was ruined for the remainder of his life. But between 1865 and 1880, he built a fortune in real estate, mines, railroads, and other economic ventures based on his business ability and his previous political career. On Brown's election to the Senate in 1880, one editor explained, "The past is dead and buried, but the future is full of hope for those who read the signs aright. The people have new interest, new hopes and new purposes. The south that Governor Brown will represent is the new south."[32]

In the same vein, B. W. Froebel, a friend of Alexander H. Stephens, explained in a letter to him that "the election of Governor Brown is an evidence of what the people really want and it's just this—they want material prosperity and whatever makes that."[33]

CHAPTER 11

Home, Church, and Last Days

Brown was always devoted to his family and his church. As he grew older, this devotion increased, and in the midst of his business ventures and his travels, he always remembered it. Indeed, many of his trips were made in the interest of his church, and whenever he could, he took his wife and some of the children along.

After Brown was officially relieved of the governorship in June 1865, his family remained in the governor's mansion in Milledgeville until December 1865, when he moved his wife and children to Atlanta. There they were welcomed to the city by the editor of the principal Atlanta paper, who believed that Brown would be successful in establishing a law practice in that city. Furthermore, the editor praised Brown's record of public service.[1]

Brown's first home in Atlanta had previously belonged to Sidney Root, a merchant who had greatly prospered in Atlanta shortly after the Civil War, but who had decided to move to New York. After Root moved, his former house on Washington Street in Atlanta was purchased by Brown, who enlarged and improved it.[2]

In the early 1870's, Brown built a new house in Atlanta on Washington Street, directly across from his old residence. The house was "a very neat and desirable one," designed with "great improvements" over any home on the street. Despite the moderate cost of the new house, it had gas lights and running water.³ Brown's old-fashioned brick home was worth about $5,000, while the grounds about the house, located on the most fashionable street in Atlanta, were valued at $50,000. Julius, his eldest son, built a large $75,000 house that adjoined and contrasted with his father's modest home.⁴

While Brown was serving as senator in Washington, he attempted to live as simply as he had in Atlanta. For a time, he had the room in the National Hotel that Henry Clay had formerly occupied. Later, Brown and his wife moved to a "modest flat on Iowa Circle." When he first went to Washington, he decided to take part in the social activities there. Since he had never worn a dress suit, he decided to order one. To protect his ailing throat, he had it made from beaver skin instead of from the usual broadcloth. But within a short time, he concluded that social activities were not for him, and he completely withdrew from them.⁵

Brown liked simple, home-cooked food. At a social gathering in Washington, he once described his favorite menu. "Well, gentlemen," he said, "you may talk of terrapin and champagne, of your sherry and your canvassbacks; you may have your crowd of boys and all that; but the best dinner on earth to me is a quiet little table with my wife and a dish of puddle duck and sweet potatoes upon it."⁶

His wife was devoted to him, and she personally kept the house and directly supervised the work done by the servants. But, despite all this, she traveled a great deal with her husband, and she also helped him with his speeches. Brown read all his Senate speeches to his wife, who aided in their composition by looking up references for him.⁷ In addition, she filled two sets of scrapbooks with clippings that dealt with her husband's career: one set contained the favorable notices of Brown; the other, the criticism of him.⁸ The children of the family helped with the scrapbooks and kept them up after their parents died, though not as efficiently as their mother had.

Of the eight children born to Brown and his wife, six were boys and two were girls.⁹ Julius, the eldest, was graduated from the University of Georgia during the Reconstruction and was admitted to the bar to practice law in 1869.[10] He went on to Harvard in 1870, where he was graduated from the Law School. He then returned to Atlanta and began his practice. It soon became a lucrative one because he served as his father's attorney in his many businesses, such as the Western & Atlantic Railroad, the Citizen's Bank, and the coal mines.

Julius had a quick temper, and in 1880, he was prevented from fighting a duel with Dr. J. G. Westmoreland by court action.[11] But, apparently, his temper did not hurt his practice, for the next year, his income was estimated at well over $20,000.[12] The expensive house that Julius built, as well as his extended trips to Cuba during the winters, show that he enjoyed spending his money.[13]

Joseph M. Brown, the second son, was graduated from Oglethorpe University with a very high academic average. Afterwards, for a short time, he attended Harvard University. He dabbled in poetry, and while he was in New England, he met Henry Wadsworth Longfellow and became somewhat infatuated with a daughter of the noted poet.[14] His extremely weak eyes prevented him from pursuing his education in law, so he went to work as a bookkeeper for the Western & Atlantic Railroad and later became superintendent of the road. After his father died, Joseph M. Brown was made a state railroad commissioner. Subsequently, he served two terms as governor of the state.

Like his brother, Julius, Elijah A. Brown attended the University of Georgia. When he finished his education, he went to work for his father as treasurer of the Dade County Coal Company. George M. Brown, the youngest member of the family, had just reached maturity when his father died. One of the daughters, Mary Virginia, married a noted Atlanta surgeon, Dr. E. L. Connally. The other daughter, Sally Eugenia Brown, never married and continued to live with her family.

Tragedy struck Brown's family twice. In 1881, his son Charles McDonald Brown died of consumption at the age of twenty-two. Before that time, another son, Franklin Pierce Brown, who was only eighteen, had died on December 16, 1871.[15] Frank suffered from a deformity of his chest and back. Walking, even with a crutch, was painful for him. Though weak in body, he had a strong mind, and his intellectual powers were sometimes compared to those of Alexander H. Stephens. As a matter of fact, the inscription on the monument over Frank's grave was taken from a letter written by Stephens to the boy's mother after his death.[16]

During Brown's later life, all of his immediate family lived in or near Atlanta. Bound by strong family ties, every Sunday his children and grandchildren gathered at his house to dine. This custom was described as a "patriarchal manner of living" and "very beautiful."[17]

On September 13, 1842, Brown had joined the Baptist church, and the Reverend Charles P. Dean had baptized him at Shady Grove Church in Pickens District in South Carolina. He remained as devoted to the Baptist church as he was to his family, and he contributed a large amount of his time, money, and talent to the work of his chosen denomination.[18]

When Brown moved to Atlanta, he and his family transferred their letters to the Second Baptist Church. The church, which was located on Washington Street across from the present site of the state capitol, had been established in 1854. During the Civil War, when Atlanta was occupied and burned by federal troops in the fall of 1864, many people had stored their personal belongings in the church. For a while, their efforts to save their household furnishings from the holocaust appeared to be futile. But the church and personal property stored there were saved by Father O'Reilly, pastor of a Catholic church in the same block. He interceded with the federal officials in behalf of the church, and they spared it. Nevertheless, services in the church were suspended until April 1865 because most of its members had fled from Atlanta.[19]

Brown, who was never a man to take a back seat in any organization with which he was connected, became active in the affairs of the Second Baptist Church shortly after he joined it. In the winter of 1866, when the churches of Atlanta combined to help the needy during the Christmas season, Brown was appointed to represent the Baptists on a committee that also included members of the Methodist, Presbyterian, Espiscopalian, and Catholic churches. As chairman of the committee, Brown proposed that speakers be asked to come to Atlanta to give a series of lectures, to which one could buy either season or single tickets. His plan was adopted, and he attempted to engage Alexander H. Stephens to give the first lecture, but Stephens declined the invitation. Nevertheless, speakers of lesser note were found, and Brown's plan for the lecture series was carried out.[20]

During the next few years, Brown served on several of his church's committees. In 1871, when its pastor, W. T. Brantley, resigned to take a church in Baltimore, Brown was made chairman of a committee that was formed to dissuade Brantley from leaving, but the committee failed in its efforts to do so.[21] Then, in 1872, at a meeting of the Georgia Baptist convention, Brown was appointed a member of the board of trustees of the orphan's home,[22] and in the same year he became a member of the Sunday School Executive Committee.[23]

Brown's interest and participation in church affairs in the 1870's increased, and in 1879, he wrote a series of seven articles on the duty of Christians to give to the *Christian Index*, the Georgia Baptist paper. Ministers, he said, neglected to talk about giving to the church and the poor, because they feared that they would be accused of selfish motives. Since he was not a minister and had no close relatives who were ministers, he felt free to discuss the subject as a layman, and "Layman" was the name with which he signed the articles.

In these articles, he quoted liberally from the Old and New Testaments.[24] The first four articles were devoted to the practice of giving to the church, and Brown said in them that he was sure that the givers would be rewarded, not only in the next world, but also in the present life.[25] When people strayed from God in Biblical times, he pointed out, they began by forgetting to tithe, and when some king tried to bring them back to God, he did so by reinstating the practice of tithing.[26]

The last three articles of the series dealt with aid to the needy. "No man stands alone," he wrote. "We are bound together by many ties, and to a great extent our interests are in common. What hurts one hurts all; what blesses one blesses all. If one has fallen, it is the interest, and duty, and privilege, and ought to be the pleasure of his neighbor, to help him up."[27] The promised rewards for such help, Brown said, were for gifts given for Christ's sake and not for gifts given for the promised rewards.[28] In cases where a person's need was doubtful, Brown believed that it was safer to "err on the side of charity, and grant, at least, some relief...."[29]

Brown practiced what he preached and gave liberally to religious organizations. No doubt, many of his gifts were not publicized, but of those that were, the $50,000 gift to the Southern Baptist Theological Seminary was the largest.

He also made generous gifts to the Second Baptist Church. At various times, he gave $500 toward its organ, $3,000 for repairs and additions to the church, and $800 toward the payment of its pastor's salary.[30] In 1890, when the church began to raise funds for a new building, Brown's name was first on the subscription list. He gave $10,000 to the building fund, and his family contributed an additional $4,000.[31]

Brown was also generous to the Baptist churches in the other localities in which he had an interest. He gave a lot near the courthouse and $225 in cash to a Baptist church in Canton, Georgia, where he had once lived.[32] In the same year, 1882, he gave several acres of ground to the Baptists in Colorado City, Texas, where he owned a large tract of land.[33]

Brown's work with the Baptist church in Georgia soon made him influential in the Southern Baptist convention. He served as one of the vice presidents of that organization from 1880 to 1884, during which time its president was Patrick Hues Mell, chancellor of the University of Georgia.[34]

In the Southern Baptist conventions, Brown took part in the discussion of discordant subjects and sometimes precipitated controversies with his remarks. When the convention met in Atlanta in May 1879, he spoke to the gathering on the unification of the Southern and Northern Baptists, for the Baptist church in this country had been divided before the Civil War by the slavery question, and that problem, Brown said, had been solved by the war. It pleased the Lord, he continued, to abolish the practice, and it had turned out to be the best for the white race. With that bone of contention removed, there was no reason why the two branches should not be unified in their purpose, their work, and their platform.[35] But Brown's proposal made no headway at this convention nor at any subsequent one.

Brown interjected an even more controversal issue into the Southern Baptist convention when it met in Augusta, Georgia in 1885, for he asked that resolutions be passed to prohibit a Baptist minister from performing a marriage ceremony if either the man or woman involved already had a living spouse. Brown made an extremely long speech in favor of his resolution, but he was stopped by the convention's president before he finished it, and the resolution failed to pass.[36]

Brown spent most of the last four years of his life in spiritual meditation. During this period, he remained at home with his family and took no part in politics except during the campaign to nominate a Democratic candidate for the presidency in 1892. Brown backed David B. Hill against Cleveland for the nomination because if Cleveland won the nomination, he would run a third time; and as Brown pointed out, using Martin Van Buren's career as an example, hitherto no candidate for a third term as president had ever been successful.[37]

Even though Brown had retired from public life, the Atlanta *Constitution* staff did not forget his birthdays. On April 15 in 1893 and in 1894, the paper carried lengthy editorials praising his past record and wishing him a happy birthday.[38] On April 15, 1894, his last birthday, he was seventy-three years of age.

For more than fifteen years, Brown had fought ill health and retirement. "The most dangerous thing a man can do is to change his habits for health's sake," he said, for when a man who was accustomed to the stress and strain of public life retired, instead of improving, he usually broke down. He had tried to keep Alexander Stephens in public office for that reason.[39]

He tried different locations and atmospheres for his ailments, as well as patent medicines and home remedies. At one time he wore a rabbit skin, minus its feet, over his chest as a protection against the cold. It worked "like a charm," he declared.[40] Nevertheless, in his last five years of life, he always rode in a closed carriage if the weather was chilly. In 1891, after Brown himself had retired, I. W. Avery said that if the senator could bc convinced that he was "just in his prime," he would not complain "of feeling sick."[41]

Brown discussed his failing health in a letter to a cousin exactly a month before he died. He was, according to the letter, in "a very sick bed;" consequently, he was unable to see the governor to ask for the appointment that the cousin desired. However, he added that he would recommend the cousin, and he told him to use the letter in any way he chose. The letter was written by someone else but signed by Brown's weak and trembling hand.[42]

When his last attack came on November 20, 1894, Brown told his family that he would not survive it. He was attended by Dr. J. C. Olmstead, the family physician, and the faithful servant Alec Kent, who had once been a servant of Alexander H. Stephens.[43] Julius remained constantly with his father and read books and papers to him.

On November 27, Brown lost consciousness and never regained it for any length of time. Three days later, his family, his servants, and his physician were summoned to his bedside, but he left no last words.[44] He died at 2:30 P. M., Friday, November 30, 1894.

"Just as a great proud ship lifts anchor and sails away to sea," reported the Atlanta *Constitution*, "did the soul of Hon. Joseph E. Brown glide away from the shores of life out upon the unknown waters whose harbor is Eternal Rest...." "It will be many a year," said an editorial in the same paper, "before Georgia can again look upon his equal—many a year before she will have a son worthy to rival him in all those high and shining qualities which make a great statesman, a leader of men, a patriot and a Christian."[45]

Likewise, the Atlanta *Journal*, which had been politically opposed to Brown ever since it was founded in 1883, carried a lengthy and flattering editorial on the deceased statesman. "He was self-reliant to a rare degree," said the editor. "His private life was above reproach." The editor concluded by saying that Georgia had "had no man who was so successful as he [Brown] both in politics and business."[46]

From the state capitol, Governor William Y. Atkinson announced Brown's death with "deep regret." By proclamation, the governor ordered that "the state flag be displayed at half-mast on the capitol and that the offices of the executive department be closed on the day appointed for his obsequies."[47] The state senate, of which Brown had once been a member, extended its sympathies to his bereaved family.[48]

News of Brown's death reached Washington, D. C. on November 30, the day it occurred. Charles F. Crisp, a congressional representative from Georgia and speaker of the house, as well as members of the Georgia congressional delegation and other friends of Brown in Washington, sent telegrams of sympathy to his family.[49]

On Sunday, December 2, the body was carried to the Georgia capitol, where it lay in state in the rotunda under a military guard. It was estimated that thousands of people "moved silently" by the body. The next morning, the body was moved from the rotunda to the house of representatives where lengthy memorial services were held.

On the afternoon of December 3, the Second Baptist Church could scarcely hold the crowds that attended Brown's funeral there.[50] The services were conducted by the Reverend Henry McDonald, pastor of the church; the Reverend A. T. Spalding, its former pastor; and the Reverend F. H. Kerfoot. Kerfoot spoke of Brown's gift to the Southern Baptist Theological Seminary and called him "its earthly savior, at the most critical period of its existence."[51] After the service, Brown was buried in the northwest corner of Oakland Cemetery in Atlanta beside the graves of the two sons who had preceded him in death. (Ironically, the father and his two sons all died on a Friday.)

Brown's extreme views were typical of those that helped to bring the war and the end of the "Old South." He was one of the makers of and contributors to the "New South." The "Old South" had been devoted to an agricultural system based on cotton culture, slave labor, and the ambition of all farmers to become plantation owners, with all the privileges and glamour of that way of life. After the Civil War a large number of conservative Southerners attempted to recreate the "Old South" by various means. Toombs was a prime example of this faction, while Brown belonged to the "New South" faction, which believed that vast changes should be made in the entire economic system of the South.

The "New South" faction advocated a change in goals for Southerners. They believed that the old cotton plantations could not be revived profitably; that farmers should raise a variety of crops which would make and save money at the same time. Farming should become a business rather than a way of life. The natural resources of the region, they believed, could be used to advantage by the development of better modes of transportation and communication. In essence, the difference between the "Old South" and the "New South" was the difference in the social goals of the one and the economic goals of the other.

There are many reasons why Brown became a leader of the "New South" faction. In the first place, he came from a mountainous area where the plantation system was not economically profitable. Although he greatly increased his holdings of agricultural land after the Civil War, they were not of the size and type to be converted into plantations.

Even before the war, it was known that the section of the state from which he came had mineral resources. While no great amount of money had been made on Georgia minerals prior to 1865, people in other parts of the nation had profited from their resources. During the war, Brown met the Waitzfelder brothers, who had business interests both in Georgia and in New York, and became their partner in the purchase of the land from the Mitchell heirs. Undoubtably, with his political acumen and his business ability, he was a welcome partner.

From these ventures, Brown moved on into different fields of business with various people. He was so keenly interested in his business ventures and his "New South" ideas that he left his life-long political party to join forces with the young businessmen and industrialists of that day. This was the unpopular thing to do during the Reconstruction, and surely a man of Brown's political ability knew it. While his change of parties ruined his political career for a time, the people he met and worked with in business helped to promote the ventures in which he was involved. Indeed, during this period, he traded his political career for one in the business world.

As a Southerner he was extremely interested in the development of the South, as well as of the nation. Education, he said on several occasions, was the key to national development. Since he was interested in economic development, it followed that he would be interested in the type of education that would further such development, and toward this end, he spent a great deal of time and money.

By 1880, Brown had accumulated a large amount of money and property. In the South, and in the nation as a whole, the majority of people had come to admire men who had climbed to the top of the economic ladder. To their way of thinking, it stood to reason that if a person could manage his own affairs successfully, then he could also successfully manage governmental affairs, and it was in this climate of political thought that Brown became a successful United States Senator.

People either hated Brown or believed implicitly in him. Given the chance, Brown could usually persuade his opponents to his point of view. Although he was not a spectacular orator, his speeches and writings proved that he could use the English language to advantage. With this ability and an uncommonly logical mind, he had a knack for making complicated subjects seem simple; sometimes, overly simple. Further, with his beard and his mannerisms, people often said he looked the part of a minister of the Gospel, and with his record of philanthropy and religious devotion, he inspired trust and confidence.

Brown's fortune was a controversial subject, both as to its amount and the ways in which it was acquired. Figures given as to the worth of his fortune varied from one and one-half million dollars to twelve million dollars. The more conservative estimate is probably nearer the more correct amount of his worth.

It has been charged that Brown made his fortune by sharp practices, if not by more dubious methods. But an unbiased examination of the available records indicates that his wealth was acquired through his business ability and political acumen. He had many enemies who would have liked to see him convicted of illegal actions, but if Brown used illegal methods to make his fortune, the court proceedings failed to prove it.

He began life under unfavorable circumstances, but he took advantage of every opportunity to gain an excellent education, and he used it to the best advantage. When the occasion presented itself, he entered politics. His name was remembered by the right people in the right places at the right time, and he became governor of Georgia.

After the war, his concentration on politics gave way to the business of accumulating a fortune. By applying his business ability and political sagacity to real estate, agriculture, railroad stocks, mines, convict labor, and other interests, he made his fortune. In 1880, he re-entered politics and crowned his political career with ten years in the United States Senate.

The Reconstruction period, then, was the turning point in Brown's life. His political career brought economic opportunities that might not have come otherwise. It is said that "opportunity knocks but once," and it seems that one knock was all Brown needed. He took advantage of every available opportunity during the Reconstruction.

Part of this chapter is reprinted with permission from the (Baptist) *Quarterly Review.*

Appendixes

GOVERNORS OF GEORGIA, 1850-1900

Howell Cobb	November 5, 1851–1853
Herschel V. Johnson	November 9, 1853–1857
Joseph E. Brown	November 6, 1857–1865
James Johnson (Provisional Governor)	June 17, 1865–1865
Charles J. Jenkins	December 14, 1865–1868
Brig. Gen. Thomas H. Ruger (Provisional Governor)	January 13, 1868–1868
Rufus B. Bullock	July 4, 1868–1871
Benjamin Conley (President of Senate)	October 30, 1871–1872
James M. Smith	January 12, 1872–1877
Alfred H. Colquitt	January 12, 1877–1882
Alexander H. Stephens	November 4, 1882–1883
James S. Boynton (President of Senate)	March 5, 1883–1883
Henry D. McDaniel	May 10, 1883–1886
John B. Gordon	November 4, 1886–1890
William J. Northen	November 8, 1890–1894
William Y. Atkinson	October 27, 1894–1898
Allen D. Candler	October 29, 1898–1902

Georgia's United States Senators
1865–1900

1865–1867—Both seats vacant.
1867–1869—Both seats vacant.
1869–1871—Joshua Hill and H. V. M. Miller
1871–1873—Joshua Hill and Thomas M. Norwood
1873–1875—Thomas M. Norwood and John B. Gordon
1875–1877—Thomas M. Norwood and John B. Gordon
1877–1879—John B. Gordon and Benjamin H. Hill
1879–1881—Benjamin H. Hill and John B. Gordon
    Joseph E. Brown (May, 1880)
1881–1883—Benjamin H. Hill and Joseph E. Brown
    M. Pope Barrow (December, 1882)
1883–1885—Joseph E. Brown and Alfred H. Colquitt
1885–1887—Joseph E. Brown and Alfred H. Colquitt
1887–1889—Joseph E. Brown and Alfred H. Colquitt
1889–1891—Joseph E. Brown and Alfred H. Colquitt
1891–1893—Alfred H. Colquitt and John B. Gordon
1893–1895—Alfred H. Colquitt and John B. Gordon
    Patrick Walsh (April, 1894)
1895–1897—John B. Gordon and Augustus O. Bacon
1897–1899—Augustus O. Bacon and Alexander S. Clay
1899–1901—Augustus O. Bacon and Alexander S. Clay

Members of the United States House of Representatives
from Georgia
1865–1895

Thirty-Ninth Congress, 1865–1867

Vacant.

Fortieth Congress, 1867–1869

Joseph W. Clift
Nelson Tift
William P. Edwards

Samuel F. Gore
Charles H. Prince
Pierce M. B. Young

Forty-First Congress, 1869–1871

William W. Paine
Richard H. Whiteley
Marion Bethune
Jefferson F. Long

Stephen Corker
William P. Price
Pierce M. B. Young

Forty-Second Congress, 1871–1873

Archibald J. MacIntyre
Richard H. Whiteley
John S. Bigby
Thomas J. Speer

Erasmus W. Beck
Dudley M. DuBose
William P. Price
Pierce M. B. Young

Forty-Third Congress, 1873–1875

Morgan Rawls
Andrew Sloan
Richard H. Whiteley
Philip Cook
Henry R. Harris

James C. Freeman
James H. Blount
Pierce M. B. Young
Alexander H. Stephens
Hiram P. Bell

Forty-Fourth Congress, 1875–1877

Julian Hartridge
William E. Smith
Philip Cook
Henry R. Harris
Milton A. Candler

James H. Blount
William H. Felton
Alexander H. Stephens
Benjamin H. Hill

Forty-Fifth Congress, 1877–1879

Julian Hartridge
William B. Fleming
William E. Smith
Philip Cook
Henry R. Harris

Milton A. Candler
James H. Blount
William H. Felton
Alexander H. Stephens
Hiram P. Bell

Forty-Sixth Congress, 1879–1881

John C. Nichols
William E. Smith

James H. Blount
William H. Felton

Philip Cook   Alexander H. Stephens
Henry Persons   Emory Speer
Nathaniel J. Hammond

Forty-Seventh Congress, 1881–1883

George R. Black   James H. Blount
Henry G. Turner   Judson C. Clements
Philip Cook   Alexander H. Stephens
Hugh Buchanan   Seaborn Reese
Nathaniel J. Hammond   Emory Speer

Forty-Eighth Congress, 1883–1885

John C. Nicholls   Thomas Hardeman
Henry G. Turner   Judson C. Clements
Charles F. Crisp   James H. Blount
Hugh Buchanan   Seaborn Reese
Nathaniel J. Hammond   Allen D. Candler

Forty-Ninth Congress, 1885–1887

Thomas M. Norwood   James H. Blount
Henry G. Turner   Judson C. Clements
Charles F. Crisp   Seaborn Reese
Henry R. Harris   Allen D. Candler
Nathaniel J. Hammond   George T. Barnes

Fiftieth Congress, 1887–1889

Thomas M. Norwood   James H. Blount
Henry G. Turner   Judson C. Clements
Charles F. Crisp   Henry H. Carlton
Thomas W. Grimes   Allen D. Candler
John D. Stewart   George T. Barnes

Fifty-First Congress, 1889–1891

Rufus E. Lester   James H. Blount
Henry G. Turner   Judson C. Clements
Charles F. Crisp   Henry H. Carlton

Thomas W. Grimes   Allen D. Candler
John D. Stewart   George T. Barnes

Fifty-Second Congress, 1891–1893

Rufus E. Lester   Thomas E. Winn
Henry G. Turner   James H. Blount
Charles F. Crisp   Robert W. Everett
Charles L. Moses   Thomas G. Lawson
Leonidas F. Livingston   Thomas E. Watson

Fifty-Third Congress, 1893–1895

Rufus E. Lester   John W. Maddox
Benjamin E. Russell   Thomas G. Lawson
Charles F. Crisp   Farish C. Tate
Charles L. Moses   James C. C. Black
Leonidas F. Livingston   Henry G. Turner
Thomas B. Cabaniss

Notes

CHAPTER 1

1. I. W. Avery, *The History of Georgia from 1850 to 1881*, pp. 7–10; Herbert Fielder, *A Sketch of The Life and Times and Speeches of Joseph E. Brown*, pp. 95–96. Brown, himself, said his ancestors came to America in 1722 and landed at Philadelphia. Joseph E. Brown to Mrs. Marie Williams, July 5, 1877, Joseph Emerson Brown Collection, University of Georgia Library.

2. Avery, *History of Georgia*, pp. 7–10; Fielder, *Joseph E. Brown*, pp. 95–96.

3. Avery, *History of Georgia*, pp. 7–10; Fielder, *Joseph E. Brown*, p. 96. See also, Samuel Boykin, *History of the Baptist Denomination in Georgia: With Biographical Compendium and Portrait Gallery of Baptist Ministers and Other Georgia Baptists*, p. 65. Boykin points out that the Pickens District of South Carolina once belonged to Georgia and was ceded to South Carolina by the Treaty of Beaufort, 1787, which gave Georgia a rather weak claim to Brown's birthplace.

4. Fielder, *Joseph E. Brown*, pp. 96–97.

5. Avery, *History of Georgia*, p. 11.

6. Fielder, *Joseph E. Brown*, pp. 97–98.

7. Avery, *History of Georgia*, p. 12; A. D. Candler, ed., *Confederate Records of the State of Georgia*, 2:207–08. During his governorship, Brown appointed Lewis superintendent of the state-owned railroad in 1857 and later senator of the Confederate states congress.

8. Candler, *Confederate Records*, 2:207–08; Avery, *History of Georgia*, p. 13.

9. Candler, *Confederate Records,* 2:207–08; Avery, *History of Georgia,* pp. 12–15.

10. Avery, *History of Georgia,* p. 14.

11. Fielder, *Joseph E. Brown,* pp. 98–101.

12. Ibid., pp. 102–07; Avery, *History of Georgia,* pp. 16–23.

13. Avery, *History of Georgia,* pp. 16–23; Fielder, *Joseph E. Brown,* pp. 98–101.

14. Avery, *History of Georgia,* pp. 16–23; Fielder, *Joseph E. Brown,* pp. 98–101.

15. Avery, *History of Georgia,* pp. 16–23; Fielder, *Joseph E. Brown,* pp. 98–101.

16. Fielder, *Joseph E. Brown,* pp. 102–07.

17. Ibid.

18. Avery, *History of Georgia,* pp. 31–46; Louise Biles Hill, *Joseph E. Brown and the Confederacy,* pp. 1–19.

19. Hill, *Joseph E. Brown,* pp. 6–8. Brown was cutting wheat on his farm in Cherokee County when he was notified of his nomination for governor.

20. Ibid., pp. 8–12.

21. Ibid., pp. 15–19. Actual fighting broke out in the Kansas Territory between anti-slavery and pro-slavery settlers there.

22. U. B. Phillips, "An American State Owned Railroad," *Yale Review,* 15:259–82.

23. Hill, *Joseph E. Brown,* pp. 15–19.

24. Ibid.

25. Ibid.

26. Horace Montgomery, *Cracker Parties,* p. 206.

27. Hill, *Joseph E. Brown,* pp. 20–24; Avery, *History of Georgia,* pp. 60–67; Fielder, *Joseph E. Brown,* pp. 119–30; Montgomery, *Cracker Parties,* pp. 211–13.

28. Hill, *Joseph E. Brown,* pp. 20–24; Avery, *History of Georgia,* pp. 60–67; Fielder, *Joseph E. Brown,* pp. 119–30; Montgomery, *Cracker Parties,* pp. 211–13.

29. Montgomery, *Cracker Parties,* pp. 206–09.

30. Hill, *Joseph E. Brown,* p. 29. Really only 77 of the 195 employees were Baptists.

31. Avery, *History of Georgia,* pp. 71–72; Fielder, *Joseph E. Brown,* pp. 130–41; Hill, *Joseph E. Brown,* pp. 26–30; Montgomery, *Cracker Parties,* pp. 211–13.

32. Avery O. Craven, *The Growth of Southern Nationalism, 1848–1861,* p. 167.

33. Fielder, *Joseph E. Brown,* pp. 146–56; Hill, *Joseph E. Brown,* pp. 25–26.
34. T. Conn Bryan, *Confederate Georgia,* p. 222.
35. Montgomery, *Cracker Parties,* pp. 213, 222, 225, 226, and 230.
36. Avery, *History of Georgia,* pp. 84–102; Hill, *Joseph E. Brown,* pp. 30–33; Montgomery, *Cracker Parties,* pp. 222–35.
37. Montgomery, *Cracker Parties,* p. 19.
38. Ibid., p. 217.
39. Hill, *Joseph E. Brown,* pp. 19 ff.
40. Montgomery, *Cracker Parties,* p. 235.

CHAPTER 2

1. Horace Montgomery, *Cracker Parties,* pp. 205, 210–11, 221.
2. Ibid., p. 238.
3. Ibid., p. 239; Louise Biles Hill, *Joseph F. Brown and the Confederacy,* p. 34.
4. Montgomery, *Cracker Parties,* pp. 241–43.
5. Ibid., pp. 243–44; T. Conn Bryan, *Confederate Georgia,* p. 1; Rudolph Von Abele, *Alexander H. Stephens, A Biography* pp. 184–85.
6. Bryan, *Confederate Georgia,* p. 3; E. Merton Coulter, *Georgia; A Short History,* p. 315–23; Hill, *Joseph E. Brown,* p. 36.
7. Montgomery, *Cracker Parties,* p. 247.
8. Von Abele, *Stephens,* p. 8.
9. Hill, *Joseph E. Brown,* p. 36; Coulter, *Georgia,* p. 319.
10. Montgomery, *Cracker Parties,* p. 249.
11. John Hope Franklin, *The Militant South, 1800–1861,* p. 188.
12. Ibid,. p. 158.
13. A. D. Candler, ed., *Confederate Records of the State of Georgia,* 2:3–5.
14. *The War of Rebellion: A Compilation of the Official Records of the Union and Confederate Armies,* ser. III, 1:7–8.
15. Ibid., p. 14.
16. Candler, *Confederate Records,* 2:5.
17. Ibid., pp. 9–17.
18. Ibid., pp. 6–8.
19. *Official Records,* series II, 2:608.
20. Coulter, *Georgia,* pp. 322–23.
21. Bryan, *Confederate Georgia,* p. 18.
22. Ibid., p. 22.
23. Hill, *Joseph E. Brown,* pp. 67–72.
24. Ibid.

25. E. Merton Coulter, *Confederate States of America, 1861–1865,* pp. 388 fn.

26. Von Abele, *Stephens,* pp. 214, 215, 219; Hill, *Joseph E. Brown,* pp. 124–37.

27. Bryan, *Confederate Georgia,* pp. 40–41.

28. Ibid., pp. 38–40.

29. Coulter, *Confederate States of America,* p. 248.

30. Ibid., p. 240.

31. Frank L. Owsley, *King Cotton Diplomacy,* pp. 48–49.

32. Albert D. Kirwan, ed., *The Confederacy,* pp. 48–49.

33. Bryan, *Confederate Georgia,* pp. 27–41; Hill, *Joseph E. Brown,* p. 107.

34. Coulter, *Confederate States of America,* p. 424.

35. *Official Records,* ser. IV, 1:597.

36. Bryan, *Confederate Georgia,* pp. 27–28.

37. Ibid., p. 38.

38. Ibid., pp. 22–26.

39. Bell Irvin Wiley, *The Life of Johnny Reb: The Common Soldier of the Confederacy,* pp. 295–96.

40. Coulter, *Confederate States of America,* p. 209.

41. Ibid., p. 114.

42. Brown to Davis, April 4, 1863, Keith Read Manuscript Collection, University of Georgia Library.

43. Coulter, *Confederate States of America,* pp. 387–88.

44. Hill, *Joseph E. Brown,* pp. 48–67; Robert Toombs to Leroy P. Walker, March 21, 1861, *Official Records,* ser. IV, 1:181; Toombs to Walker, March 23, 1861, *Official Records* ser. IV, 1:184. In addition to Secretary of War Leroy Walker, Brown wrote stinging letters to President Jefferson Davis and Walker's successors in the War Department.

45. Coulter, *Confederate States of America,* p. 312.

46. Kirwan, *The Confederacy,* pp. 198–201.

47. Brown to Randolph, May 26, 1862, *Official Records,* ser. IV, 1:1128–29.

48. Hill, *Joseph E. Brown,* pp. 79–106; Bryan, *Confederate Georgia,* pp. 85–95.

49. Coulter, *Confederate States of America,* p. 268.

50. Bell Irvin Wiley, *Southern Negroes, 1861–1865,* pp. 118–21.

51. Hill, *Joseph E. Brown,* pp. 162–93.

52. Coulter, *Confederate States of America,* p. 541.

53. Hill, *Joseph E. Brown,* pp. 194–221.

54. Ibid., pp. 138–61.
55. Coulter, *Confederate States of America*, pp. 176–77.
56. Ibid., pp. 292–93.
57. Ibid., p. 540.
58. Ibid., p. 539.
59. Ibid., p. 542; Coulter, *Georgia*, p. 342.
60. Hill, *Joseph E. Brown*, p. 239.
61. Coulter, *Confederate States of America*, p. 554.
62. Ibid.
63. Coulter, *Georgia*, p. 325.

CHAPTER 3

1. Brown to Alexander H. Stephens, April 25, 1865, U. B. Phillips, ed., *The Correspondence of Robert Toombs, Alexander H. Stephens and Howell Cobb*. p. 662.
2. J. H. Wilson to Brown, April 27, 1865, Joseph Emerson Brown Collection, University of Georgia Library.
3. Wilson to Brown, April 28, 1865, A. D. Candler, ed., *Confederate Records of the State of Georgia*, 3:714.
4. Brown to Wilson, April 28, 1865, Candler, *Confederate Records*, 3:714.
5. Sherman to the generals under his command, *The War of the Rebellion: A Compilation of the Official Records of the Union and Confederate Armies*, ser. I, 49, pt. 2:485–86.
6. Wilson to Brown, May 3, 1865, Candler, *Confederate Records*, 3:715–16.
7. Henry C. Wayne to Wilson, May 4, and 5, 1865, Candler, *Confederate Records*, 3:716–17.
8. Typescript copy of parole, Joseph E. Brown Collection, University of Georgia Library.
9. *Milledgeville Confederate Union*, May 9, 1865.
10. Brown to President Andrew Johnson, May 6, 1865, *Official Records*, ser. I, 49, pt. 2:630.
11. Edwin M. Stanton to Wilson, May 7, 1865, *Official Records*, ser. I, 49, pt. 2:646–47; Candler, *Confederate Records* 3:719–21; *Augusta Chronicle and Sentinel*, May 16, 1865; Wilson to Brown, May 9, 1865, *Official Records*, ser. I, 49, pt. 2:681–82.
12. Stanton to Wilson, May 7, 1865, *Official Records*, ser. I, 49, pt. 2:647.
13. Ibid., p. 648.

14. Wilson to Stanton, May 9, 1865, *Official Records*, ser. I, 49, pt. 2:680. See also, Special Order No. 73, *Official Records*, ser. I, 49, pt. 2:683.

15. Joseph E. Brown to Johnson, May 20, 1865, Joseph Emerson Brown Collection, University of Georgia Library.

16. Grant to Stanton, May 19, 1865, *Official Records*, ser. I, 49, pt. 2:836.

17. Grant to Stanton, May 20, 1865, *Official Records*, ser. I, 49, pt. 2:847.

18. *Savannah Daily Herald*, May 19, 1865.

19. Ibid., May 26, 1865.

20. Ibid., May 30, 1865.

21. Special Order No. 74, *Official Records*, ser. I, 49, pt. 2:703.

22. William Hidell to Linton Stephens, May 14, 1865, Alexander H. Stephens Collection, Sacred Heart College Library, Manhattanville, N. Y. Microfilm in the University of Georgia Library.

23. General E. B. Beaumont to General E. F. Winslow, May 10, 1865, Alexander H. Stephens Collection, Sacred Heart College Library, Manhattanville, N. Y. Microfilm in the University of Georgia Library.

24. General William D. Whipple to General Charles Cruft, May 13, 1865, *Official Records*, ser. I, 49, pt. 3:753.

25. Ibid., May 15, 1865, *Official Records*, ser. I, 49, pt. 3:792.

26. General Howell Cobb to Mrs. Howell Cobb, May 25, 1865, Howell Cobb Collection, University of Georgia Library.

27. *Savannah Daily Herald*, May 25, 1865.

28. Brown to Johnson, May 20, 1865. Typescript copy, Joseph Emerson Brown Collection, University of Georgia Library.

29. Ibid., May 21, 1865, Joseph Emerson Brown Collection, University of Georgia Library.

30. Ibid.

31. Ibid.

32. Ibid.

33. Ibid.

34. Ibid.

35. Pass from President Johnson to Brown, May 29, 1865, Joseph Emerson Brown Collection, University of Georgia Library. See also, Brown to Johnson, May 23, 1865, Joseph E. Brown Papers, Felix Hargrett Collection, University of Georgia Library.

36. *Savannah Daily Herald*, June 8, 1865; Candler, *Confederate Records of Georgia*, 3:799.

37. Typescript copy of parole, Joseph Emerson Brown Collection, University of Georgia Library.
38. Brown to Mrs. Brown, June 3, 1865, Candler, *Confederate Records,* 3:729.
39. *Savannah Daily Herald,* June 7, 1865.
40. *Augusta Chronicle and Sentinel,* June 14, 1865.
41. Ibid., June 11, 1865.
42. *Savannah Daily Herald,* June 15, 1865.
43. *Augusta Chronicle and Sentinel,* June 21, 1865.
44. *Milledgeville Federal Union,* July 11, 1865.

CHAPTER 4

1. *Augusta Chronicle and Sentinel,* July 16, 1865.
2. *Milledgeville Federal Union,* July 11, 1865.
3. General J. H. Wilson to General George H. Thomas, July 2, 1865, *The War of Rebellion: A Compilation of the Official Records of the Union and Confederate Armies,* ser. I, 49, pt. 2:1060.
4. Thomas to Wilson, July 4, 1865, *Official Records,* ser. I, 49, pt. 2:1064.
5. *Milledgeville Federal Union,* July 25, 1865.
6. *Augusta Chronicle and Sentinel,* August 9, 1865.
7. Ibid., August 6, 1865.
8. Brown to Johnson, July 21, 1865, *Official Records,* ser. I, 49, pt. 2:1088.
9. Johnson to Brown, July 25, 1865, A. D. Candler, *Confederate Records of the State of Georgia,* 3:73.
10. C. Mildred Thompson, *Reconstruction in Georgia,* pp. 144–45.
11. *Milledgeville Federal Union,* August 23, 1865.
12. *Augusta Chronicle and Sentinel,* September 6, 1865. Alexander Stephens was released October 12, 1865. Rudolph Von Abele, *Alexander H. Stephens, A Biography,* p. 255.
13. Brown's oath, September 5, 1865, Joseph Emerson Brown Collection, University of Georgia Library.
14. Brown's Pardon, September 6, 1865, Joseph Emerson Brown Collection, University of Georgia Library.
15. Brown's Pardon Acceptance, September 6, 1865, Joseph Emerson Brown Collection, University of Georgia Library.
16. *Milledgeville Federal Union,* September 19, 1865.
17. *Atlanta Intelligencer,* September 13, 1865.
18. *Savannah Daily Herald,* September 12, 1865.

19. Ibid., September 25, 1865.

20. *Augusta Chronicle and Sentinel*, September 20, 1865.

21. *Milledgeville Federal Union*, May 29, 1866.

22. Thompson, *Reconstruction in Georgia*, p. 145.

23. Candler, *Confederate Records*, 4:160.

24. *Milledgeville Federal Union*, October 10, 1865.

25. Ibid., November 7, 1865.

26. *Augusta Chronicle and Sentinel*, November 8, 1865.

27. *Milledgeville Federal Union*, November 21, 1865.

28. Joseph E. Brown to A. H. Stephens, November 9, 1865, Alexander H. Stephens Papers, Emory University Library; U. B. Phillips, *The Correspondence of Robert Toombs, Alexander H. Stephens and Howell Cobb*, pp. 670–71.

29. J. B. Dumble to A. H. Stephens, November 17, 1865, A. H. Stephens Papers, Emory University Library.

30. Brown to A. H. Stephens, November 9, 1865, Alexander H. Stephens Papers, Emory University Library; Phillips, *Toombs, Stephens and Cobb*, pp. 670–71.

31. Linton Stephens to A. H. Stephens, November 20, 1865, Alexander H. Stephens Papers, College of the Sacred Heart Library, Manhattanville, N. Y. On microfilm in the University of Georgia Library.

32. Brown to A. H. Stephens, November 9, 1865, Alexander H. Stephens Papers, Emory University Library; Phillips, *Toombs, Stephens and Cobb*, pp. 670–71.

33. L. Stephens to A. H. Stephens, November 20, 1865, Alexander H. Stephens Papers, College of the Sacred Heart Library. On Microfilm in the University of Georgia Library.

34. Brown to Johnson, January 31, 1866, *Atlanta Constitution*, November 15, 1877.

35. Fielder, Herbert, *A Sketch of the Life and Times and Speeches of Joseph E. Brown* p. 47.

36. Ezekial Waitzfelder was one of this pair of brothers with whom Brown entered into some business ventures. In a letter to Brown, Charles H. Reid, a London businessman wrote that Leopold Waitzfelder attempted to collect some money from the Reid Company in Brown's name. The money was in an account of the State of Georgia. Reid refused to pay and threatened to expose the affair to Georgia authorities. Charles H. Reid to Brown, October 3, 1865, Joseph Emerson Brown Papers, Felix Hargrett Collection, University of Georgia Library.

37. E. Starnes to C. J. Jenkins, January 19, 1866, Telamon Cuyler Collection, University of Georgia Library.

38. *Milledgeville Federal Union*, March 6, 1866.

39. *The Christian Index*, March 29, 1866.

40. *Augusta Chronicle and Sentinel*, February 24, 1866.

41. Ibid., February 20, 1866; *Milledgeville Federal Union*, February 20, 1866; Thompson, *Reconstruction in Georgia*, p. 157.

42. Thompson, *Reconstruction in Georgia*, p. 157.

43. Brown to Stephens, April 26, 1866, Alexander H. Stephens Papers, Emory University Library.

44. *Milledgeville Federal Union*, May 29, 1866.

45. *Lawyers Test Oath, United States District Court, Southern District of Georgia, May Term, 1866, Ex Parte William Law. Argument of Honorable Henry S. Fitch, United States District Attorney*, p. 22.

46. Brown to Stephens, May 17, 1866, Alexander H. Stephens Papers, Emory University Library.

47. *Opinion of Honorable John Erskine, United States District Court of Georgia, in Ex Parte William Law Case*, p. 29.

CHAPTER 5

1. I. W. Avery. *The History of Georgia, from 1850 to 1881*, p. 363.

2. *Atlanta Intelligencer*, February 27, 1867.

3. Brown to A. K. Seago *et al*, February 23, 1867, *Milledgeville Federal Union*, March 5, 1867.

4. Ibid.

5. Ibid.

6. Ibid.

7. Ibid.

8. Ibid.

9. Ibid.

10. *Atlanta Intelligencer*, March 13, 1867.

11. *Milledgeville Federal Union*, March 5, 1867.

12. *Augusta Constitutionalist*, March 6, 1867.

13. *Atlanta Intelligencer*, March 13, 1867.

14. Ibid.

15. *Thomasville Southern Enterprise*, March 1, 1867.

16. Brown to D. Wilkinson, *Atlanta Intelligencer*, April 8, 1867; Brown Scrapbook, 1866–67, Joseph Emerson Brown Collection, University of Georgia Library.

17. *Atlanta Intelligencer*, May 1, 1867; *Milledgeville Federal Union*, May 7, 1867.

18. *Milledgeville Federal Union*, June 6, 1867.

19. Robert Toombs to Stephens, June 14, 1867, Alexander H. Stephens Papers, Emory University Library.

20. James W. Hunnicutt, a Virginia Radical was born in South Carolina and went to Virginia as a preacher and editor. He once owned slaves and later voted for secession. During Reconstruction, he advised Negroes to steal food and use violence when it might be effective. See Claude G. Bowers, *The Tragic Era: The Revolution After Lincoln* (Boston, 1929), pp. 199–200.

21. *Cincinnati Commercial,* May 7, 1867, Brown Scrapbook, Joseph Emerson Brown Collection, University of Georgia Library.

22. Louise Biles Hill, *Joseph E. Brown and the Confederacy,* pp. 272 ff.

23. "Notes on the Situation," *Augusta Chronicle and Sentinel,* June 19 to August 1, 1867; Brown Scrapbook, Joseph Emerson Brown Collection, University of Georgia Library; DeRenne Collection, University of Georgia Library.

24. *Augusta Chronicle and Sentinel,* June 19 to August 1, 1867; Brown Scrapbook, Joseph Emerson Brown Collection, University of Georgia Library; DeRenne Collection, University of Georgia Library.

25. *Augusta Chronicle and Sentinel,* June 19 to August 1, 1867; Brown Scrapbook, Joseph Emerson Brown Collection, University of Georgia Library; DeRenne Collection, University of Georgia Library.

26. *Milledgeville Federal Union,* August 13, 1867.

27. *Augusta Chronicle and Sentinel,* August 1, 1867.

28. Brown's "Review of Notes on the Situation," *Augusta Chronicle and Sentinel,* August 1 to August 9, 1867; Brown Scrapbook, Joseph Emerson Brown Collection, University of Georgia Library.

29. Brown's "Review of Notes on the Situation," *Augusta Chronicle and Sentinel,* August 1 to August 9, 1867; Brown Scrapbook, Joseph Emerson Brown Collection, University of Georgia Library.

30. *Augusta Chronicle and Sentinel,* August 1 to August 9, 1867; Brown Scrapbook, Joseph Emerson Brown Collection, University of Georgia Library.

31. The decision on Negro officeholders came while Brown was chief justice of the Supreme Court of Georgia.

32. *Milledgeville Federal Union,* January 21, 1868.

CHAPTER 6

1. *Congressional Globe,* 1st Session, 40th Congress, Part II, p. 118.

2. *Thomasville Southern Enterprise,* March 19, 1867. G. W. Ashburn, a Radical in Columbus, Georgia, was later killed by a mob in that city.

3. *Augusta Constitutionalist,* July 1, 1868.

4. *Georgia Weekly Opinion* (Atlanta), January 14, 1868.

5. *Atlanta Constitution,* June 19, 1868.

6. *Daily New Era* (Atlanta), March 11, 1868. Brown Scrapbook, 1868–72, Joseph Emerson Brown Collection, University of Georgia Library.

7. Brown to Stephens, June 7, 1870, Alexander H. Stephens Papers, Library of Congress, Washington, D. C.

8. *Brown's Speech to the Republican Convention,* May 20, 1868, DeRenne Collection, University of Georgia Library.

9. Ibid.

10. Ibid.

11. Ibid.

12. *Augusta Constitutionalist,* June 10, 1868.

13. Ibid., June 3, 1868.

14. *Atlanta Constitution,* August 8, 1868.

15. *Milledgeville Federal Union,* May 29, 1866.

16. *Columbus Sun,* August 20, 1868.

17. *Daily New Era* (Atlanta), March 11, 1868; Brown Scrapbook, 1868–72, Joseph Emerson Brown Collection, University of Georgia Library.

18. *Daily New Era* (Atlanta), March 11, 1868; Brown Scrapbook, 1868–72, Joseph Emerson Brown Collection, University of Georgia Library.

19. *Speech of Joseph E. Brown at Marietta,* March 18, 1868, pp. 1–8.

20. *Georgia Opinion* (Atlanta), April 7, 1868.

21. *Columbus Sun,* March 13, 1868. Brown owned a complete block of business buildings in downtown Atlanta, and the five-story building was one of the largest in the city.

22. Ibid., March 22, 1868. W. G. Brownlow was a Tennessee Unionist.

23. C. Mildred Thompson, *Reconstruction in Georgia,* pp. 204–09.

24. *Atlanta Constitution,* July 15, 1868.

25. Ibid., July 17, 1868.

26. Ibid., July 26, 1868.

27. Ibid., July 29, 1868.

28. *Augusta Chronicle and Sentinel,* August 8, 1868.

29. Brown Scrapbook, 1868–72, Joseph Emerson Brown Collection, University of Georgia Library.

30. *Atlanta Constitution,* July 30, 1868.

31. Ibid.; *Augusta Constitutionalist,* August 5, 1868.

32. Robert Toombs to Alexander H. Stephens, August 9, 1868, U.

B. Phillips, *The Correspondence of Robert Toombs, Alexander H. Stephens and Howell Cobb*, p. 703.

33. *Atlanta Constitution*, August 2, 1868.
34. Ibid., August 4, 1868.
35. Ibid., June 27, 1868.
36. Ibid., June 28, 1868.
37. Ibid., August 30, 1868.
38. I. W. Avery, *History of Georgia from 1850 to 1881*, p. 399–400.
39. *Atlanta Constitution*, September 16, 1868.

CHAPTER 7

1. *Milledgeville Federal Union*, February 26, 1867; *The Christian Index*, February 21, 1867.
2. *Columbus Sun*, April 1, 1868.
3. U. S. Grant to George G. Meade, April 2, 1868, *Major General Meade's Report on the Ashburn Murder*, p. 28.
4. Meade to General John M. Schofield, June 26, 1868, *Major General Meade's Report on the Ashburn Murder*, p. 33.
5. Schofield to Meade, June 27, 1868, *Major General Meade's Report on the Ashburn Murder*, p. 34.
6. *Atlanta Constitution*, June 19, 1868.
7. *Augusta Constitutionalist*, June 24, 1868.
8. *Atlanta Constitution*, June 20, 1868.
9. Ibid., July 12, 1868.
10. Ibid., July 11, 1868; Columbus *Sun*, July 24, 1868.
11. *Columbus Sun*, July 11, 1868.
12. Nancy Telfair, *A History of Columbus, Georgia, 1828–1928*, p. 164–66.
13. Meade to Schofield and U. S. Grant, June 30, 1868, *Major General Meade's Report on the Ashburn Murder*, p. 35.
14. *Atlanta Constitution*, July 23, 1868.
15. *Joseph E. Brown and the Columbus Prisoners*, p. 1–16.
16. *Atlanta Constitution*, September 24, 1879.
17. Ibid., September 25, 1879.
18. Ibid., September 26, 1879.
19. Ibid., October 7, 1879. To illustrate his accusation that Brown perverted facts, Garrard quoted Campbell Wallace as saying, "If I were to catch Joseph E. Brown in the dead of the night in my chicken house, with some of my chickens already taken off and tied, and he started

off with them in his hand, I would so fear that he would charge me and prove that I had stolen my own chickens, that I would say to him, 'Now Governor we are both in a bad scrape together, and if you will only take the chickens and say nothing about it, we will drop the matter right here.' "

20. Ibid., October 2, 1879.

21. Ibid., October 3, 1879. Cases mentioned were Cody of Warren and Digby of Jasper.

22. Ibid., October 1, 1879.

23. Ibid., October 4, 1879.

24. Ibid., November 2, 1879.

25. Ibid.

26. *Mountain Chronicle*, (Dawsonville), October 7, 1879; Brown Scrapbook, 1879, Joseph Emerson Brown Collection, University of Georgia Library.

27. *Atlanta Constitution*, November 2, 1879.

28. Brown to L. N. Trammell, September 24, 1879, L. N. Trammell Papers, Emory University Library.

29. Meade to Schofield and U. S. Grant, June 30, 1868, *Major General Meade's Report on the Ashburn Murder*, p. 35.

30. *Columbus Sun*, August 8, 1868.

31. C. Mildred Thompson, *Reconstruction in Georgia*, pp. 354–55.

32. *Atlanta Constitution*, August 13, 1868; Bullock's nomination of Brown, "Executive Minutes of the State of Georgia, 1866–70," Georgia State Department of Archives and History, Atlanta, Georgia, p. 163.

33. Brown's Chief Justice Commission, Joseph Emerson Brown Collection, University of Georgia Library.

34. *Columbus Sun*, August 14, 1868.

35. *Augusta Chronicle and Sentinel*, August 21, 1868.

36. *Atlanta Constitution*, August 22, 1868.

37. *Joseph E. Brown's Speech at Marietta, March 18, 1868*, pp. 1–8.

38. E. Merton Coulter, *Georgia, A Short History*, p. 370.

39. *Can a Negro Hold Office in Georgia? Arguments of Counsel with Opinions of the Judges and the Decision of the Court in the Case of Richard W. White, Clerk of the Superior Court of Chatham County, Plaintiff in Error, versus the State of Georgia, ex relatione William J. Clements, Defendant in Error. Quo warranto. Chatham*, pp. 8–17.

40. Ibid., pp. 112–15; *Atlanta Constitution*, June 17, 1868.

41. *Can a Negro Hold Office in Georgia?*, p. 125.

42. *Augusta Chronicle and Sentinal*, June 16, 1869.

43. *Savannah Morning News,* June 16, 1869.

44. Stephens to A. R. Wright, June 29, 1869, *Can a Negro Hold Office in Georgia?* pp. 168–71.

45. Ibid.

46. Coulter, *Georgia,* p. 373.

47. "State of Georgia Executive Minutes, 1866–70," Georgia State Department of Archives and History, Atlanta, Georgia, p. 679.

48. Brown to Governor Rufus B. Bullock, December 24, 1870, *Atlanta Constitution,* December 27, 1870.

CHAPTER 8

1. Brown to Alexander Stephens, December 27, 1869, Alexander H. Stephens Papers, Library of Congress, Washington, D.C.

2. Brown to Stephens, January 4, 1870, Alexander H. Stevens Papers, Library of Congress, Washington, D.C.

3. C. Mildred Thompson, *Reconstruction in Georgia,* p. 258.

4. Brown to I. W. Avery, January 1, 1870, *Atlanta Constitution,* January 5, 1870; *Milledgeville Federal Union,* January 11, 1870.

5. Brown to I. W. Avery, January 1, 1870, *Atlanta Constitution,* January 5, 1870.

6. Ibid.

7. Ibid.

8. Ibid.

9. *Milledgeville Federal Union,* January 11, 1870.

10. *Atlanta Constitution,* January 12, 1870.

11. Robert Toombs to A. H. Stephens, January 24, 1870, U. B. Phillips, ed., *The Correspondence of Robert Toombs, Alexander H. Stephens and Howell Cobb,* p. 707.

12. *Atlanta Constitution,* October 31, 1871. A joint resolution criticizing the manner of Bullock's resignation, *Georgia Laws,* 1871–72, pp. 263–64.

13. *Athens Southern Watchman* quoted by the *Atlanta Constitution,* January 19, 1872.

14. Linton Stephens to A. H. Stephens, January 11, 1872, Alexander H. Stephens Papers, College of the Sacred Heart, Manhattanville, N.Y.

15. *Atlanta Constitution,* April 26, 1872. Brown, at the time the convention met, was taking part in the Georgia Baptist convention in Macon.

16. Ibid., July 25, 1872.

17. Ibid.

18. Brown to John L. Hull, September 13, 1872, *Atlanta Constitution,* September 24, 1872.

19. Ibid.
20. Ibid.
21. Ibid., October 22, 1872.
22. Brown to the *Atlanta Constitution*, August 5, 1872, *Atlanta Constitution*, August 22, 1872. See also, *Atlanta Constitution*, September 1, October 14, 1840; *Senate Journal*, pt. 3, 1870, pp. 523, 550–52.
23. *Atlanta Constitution*, August 5, 1872.
24. Ibid., July 3, 1873.
25. Ibid.
26. Ibid., July 17, 1872.
27. Ibid., July 18, 1872.
28. *The Hatchet* (Washington, D.C.), May 9, 1886; Brown Scrapbook, 1885–86, Joseph Emerson Brown Collection, University of Georgia Library.
29. Pleasant A. Stovall, *Robert Toombs, Statesman, Speaker, Soldier, Sage*, p. 335.
30. *Augusta Chronicle and Sentinel*, July, 1872.
31. Benjaman Barrow to Colonel D. C. Barrow, November 6, 1872, Colonel David C. Barrow Collection, University of Georgia Library.
32. Stovall, *Toombs*, pp. 335–36.
33. *Atlanta Constitution*, February 13, 1873.
34. Ibid., September 6, 1874.
35. Ibid.
36. Ibid.
37. Ibid.
38. *Albany News*, September 24, 1874; Brown Scrapbook, 1874–76, Joseph Emerson Brown Collection, University of Georgia Library.
39. *Atlanta Constitution*, October 14, 1874.

CHAPTER 9

1. *Atlanta Constitution*, October 31, 1876. A portion of this chapter is reprinted with permission from *Florida Historical Quarterly*.
2. William Watson Davis, *The Civil War and Reconstruction in Florida*, pp. 687–712.
3. *Atlanta Constitution*, November 13, 1876.
4. Ibid.
5. Brown Scrapbook, 1875–78, Joseph Emerson Brown Collection, University of Georgia Library. No title nor date.
6. *Atlanta Constitution*, November 16, 1876.
7. Ibid., November 18, 1876. Grady and his partners published

the *Atlanta Herald*. After some derogatory remarks concerning Brown, early in 1876, the Citizens Bank in Atlanta, of which Brown was a large stockholder, foreclosed on a mortgage given by the paper, thus putting it out of existence.

   8. Ibid.

   9. Ibid.

  10. Ibid., November 25, 1876.

  11. Ibid., November 29, 1876.

  12. Ibid., November 30, 1876.

  13. Ibid., December 1, 1876.

  14. Ibid., December 6, 1876.

  15. Ibid., December 7, 1876.

  16. Ibid.

  17. Ibid., December 8, 1876.

  18. Ibid., December 9, 1876.

  19. Ibid., December 10, 1876.

  20. Brown to L. N. Trammell, December 12, 1876, L. N. Trammell Papers, Emory University Library.

  21. *Atlanta Constitution*, December 13, 1876.

  22. Brown to E. Y. Clarke *et al*, December 12, 1876, *Atlanta Constitution*, December 13, 1876.

  23. *Augusta Chronicle and Sentinel*, November 26, 1876.

  24. *Atlanta Constitution*, December 7, 1876.

  25. Ibid., December 9, 1876.

  26. *Rome* (Georgia) *Evening News*, December 15, 1876; Brown Scrapbook, 1875–78, Joseph Emerson Brown Collection, University of Georgia Library.

  27. Brown to L. N. Trammell, December 12, 1876, L. N. Trammell Papers, Emory University Library.

  28. C. Vann Woodward, *Origins of the New South, 1877–1912*, p. 23–50. See also, C. Vann Woodward *Reunion and Reaction: The Compromise of 1877 and the End of Reconstruction* (Boston, 1951).

  29. *Atlanta Constitution*, April 7, 1877; *Atlanta Constitution*, April 22, 1877.

  30. *Atlanta Constitution*, April 7, 1877; *Atlanta Constitution*, April 22, 1877.

  31. *Atlanta Constitution* April 22, 1877.

  32. Ibid., May 2, 1877.

  33. Ibid.

  34. E. L. Connally to Brown, May 20, 1877, Joseph Emerson Brown Collection, University of Georgia Library.

35. *New Orleans Democrat,* quoted by the *Athens Georgian,* May 22, 1877.

36. *Atlanta Constitution,* March 14, 1877.

37. Ibid., June 5, 1877.

38. Ibid., June 12, 1877.

39. Ibid., June 13, 1877.

40. E. L. Connally to Brown, May 30, 1877, Joseph Emerson Brown Collection, University of Georgia Library.

41. Brown to L. N. Trammell, December 12, 1876, L. N. Trammell Papers, Emory University Library.

42. *Atlanta Constitution,* April 1, 1876.

43. *Rome* (Georgia) *Evening News,* December 15, 1876; Brown Scrapbook, 1875–78, Joseph Emerson Brown Collection, University of Georgia Library.

44. *Cleveland* (Georgia) *Advertiser,* April 12, 1880; Brown Scrapbook, 1875–78, Joseph Emerson Brown Collection, University of Georgia Library.

45. *Marietta Journal,* August 28, 1879; *Cleveland* (Georgia) *Advertiser,* April 12, 1880.

46. *Atlanta Constitution,* December 23, 1876.

47. *Augusta Constitutionalist,* January 5, 1877; Brown Scrapbook, 1875–78, Joseph Emerson Brown Collection, University of Georgia Library.

48. *Atlanta Constitution,* January 26, 1877.

49. *LaGrange Reporter,* quoted by the *Atlanta Constitution,* January 7, 1877.

50. *Gainesville Southron,* October 12, 1875; Brown Scrapbook, 1874–76, Joseph Emerson Brown Collection, University of Georgia Library.

51. *Monroe Advertiser,* n.d.; Brown Scrapbook, 1880, Joseph Emerson Brown Collection, University of Georgia Library.

CHAPTER 10

1. *Augusta Chronicle and Sentinel,* October 13, 1870.

2. *Testimony of the Legislative Investigation of the Lease of the Western & Atlantic Railroad, 1872,* pp. 118–155; *Acts of the General Assembly of the State of Georgia, 1870,* pp. 423–27.

3. *Testimony of the Legislative Investigation,* pp. 172–93.

4. Ibid.; see also, *House Journal of the Georgia General Assembly, 1876,* p. 682 and *Report of the Joint Committee of the General Assembly to Investigate the Western & Atlantic Railroad, 1880–81.*

5. *Atlanta Constitution,* June 2, 1886.

6. *Ellijay Courier,* November 8, 1886, Brown Scrapbook, 1886–87, Joseph Emerson Brown Collection, University of Georgia Library.

7. *Atlanta Constitution,* April 3, 1878.

8. Ibid., June 28, 1890.

9. *Georgia Laws, 1890–91,* pp. 533–37.

10. Ibid., p. 280.

11. "Executive Minutes of the State of Georgia, 1890–91," Georgia State Department of Archives and History, Atlanta, Georgia, p. 250.

12. *Atlanta Constitution,* February 12, 1891.

13. Ibid., May 24, 1891.

14. *Georgia Laws, 1873,* pp. 185–86.

15. *House Journal, 1874,* p. 363; and *Georgia Laws, 1874,* pp. 274–88.

16. *Gazette,* September 14, 1879, Brown Scrapbook, Joseph Emerson Brown Collection, University of Georgia Library. See also, *Atlanta Constitution,* May 18, 1873.

17. Derrell Roberts, "Joseph E. Brown and the Convict Lease System," *Georgia Historical Quarterly* (December, 1960), 44:399–410.

18. *The Citizen* (Dalton, Georgia), September 20, 1883; Brown Scrapbooks, Joseph Emerson Brown Collection, University of Georgia Library.

19. *Congressional Record, Forty-Eighth Congress, Second Session,* 18, pt. 4:4011–14.

20. An unidentified clipping with the dateline of Canton, Georgia, June 21, 1905, Brown Scrapbooks, Joseph Emerson Brown Collection, University of Georgia Library.

21. Brown to Mark Bransford and B. A. Thornton, April 26, 1892; *Atlanta Constitution,* May 15, 1892.

22. Brown to Mark Bransford and B. A. Thornton, April 26, 1892; *Atlanta Constitution,* May 15, 1892.

23. Brown to Mark Bransford and B. A. Thornton, April, 26, 1892; *Atlanta Constitution,* May 15, 1892.

24. Derrell Roberts, "Joseph E. Brown and the University of Georgia," *The Georgia Review,* 19 (Summer, 1965): 239–43.

25. Ibid., 243–50.

26. B. D. Ragsdale, *The Story of Georgia Baptists,* 1:186–200; *Atlanta Constitution,* May 11, July 2, and August 18, 1870.

27. William A. Mueller, *A History of Southern Baptist Theological Seminary* pp. 46, 229; *The Christian Index,* April 1 and 8, 1880.

28. Derrell Roberts, "Joseph E. Brown and the Atlanta Public Schools," *Peabody Journal of Education,* 43:42–49.

29. Ibid. See also, *Atlanta Constitution,* August 31, 1873.

30. Derrell Roberts, "Joseph E. Brown and the Atlanta Public Schools," *Peabody Journal of Education*, 43:42–49; *Atlanta Constitution*, August 31, 1873.

31. In addition to the *Congressional Record* of the period, there is a good collection of Brown's speeches in the DeRenne Collection in the University of Georgia Library. See also, Leona Speers, "The Senatorial Career of Joseph E. Brown," M.A. thesis presented to the University of Georgia at Athens, Georgia, 1954; Judson C. Ward, "Georgia Under the Bourbon Democrats, 1872–1890," Ph. D. dissertation presented to the University of North Carolina at Chapel Hill, North Carolina, 1947.

32. *Atlanta Constitution*, November 17, 1880.

33. B. W. Froebel to Alexander H. Stephens, December 4, 1880, Alexander H. Stephens Collection, Library of Congress, Washington, D. C.

CHAPTER 11

1. *Atlanta Intelligencer*, January 10, 1866.

2. B. D. Ragsdale, *The Story of Georgia Baptists*, 1:183.

3. *Atlanta Constitution*, August 24, 1871.

4. *Evening Star* (Washington, D. C.), January 29, 1887; Brown Scrapbook, 1868–1937, Joseph Emerson Brown Collection, University of Georgia Library.

5. *New York World*, October (n.d.), 1890; Brown Scrapbook, 1889–91, Joseph Emerson Brown Collection, University of Georgia Library.

6. Ibid.

7. Ibid.

8. An unidentified clipping dated February 21, 1888, Brown Scrapbook, 1888, Joseph Emerson Brown Collection, University of Georgia Library.

9. Diagram of Brown family tree, Joseph Emerson Brown Collection, University of Georgia Library.

10. *Atlanta Constitution*, September 7, 1869.

11. Ibid., September 17, 18, 19, 1880.

12. Ibid., November 19, 1881.

13. *Evening Star* (Washington, D. C.), January 29, 1887; Brown Scrapbook, 1868–1937, Joseph Emerson Brown Collection, University of Georgia Library.

14. Walter R. Brown to Joseph M. Brown, December 7, 1873, Joseph M. Brown Collection, University of Georgia Library.

15. *Atlanta Constitution*, December 17 and 19, 1871.

16. Joseph E. Brown to Alexander Stephens, January 7, 1872, Alexander H. Stephens Collection, Library of Congress, Washington, D. C.

17. *Atlanta Evening Herald*, February 18, 1891; Brown Scrapbook, 1890–92, Joseph Emerson Brown Collection, University of Georgia Library.

18. Samuel Boykin, *History of the Baptist Denomination in Georgia: With Biographical Compendium and Portrait Gallery of Baptist Ministers and Other Georgia Baptists*, pp. 65–68

19. Mrs. John S. Spalding, "The Second Baptist Church," *Atlanta Historical Bulletin*, 8 (October, 1945): 37–38.

20. Brown to Stephens, December 8, 1866, U. B. Phillips, ed., *The Correspondence of Robert Toombs, Alexander H. Stephens and Howell Cobb*, pp. 684–85; Brown to Stephens, December 20, 1866, Alexander H. Stephens Collection, Emory University Library.

21. *Atlanta Constitution*, July 10, 1871.

22. "Minutes of the Georgia Baptist Convention, April 26, 1872," Mercer University Library, Macon, Georgia.

23. *Atlanta Constitution*, April 27, 1872.

24. *The Christian Index*, March 6, 1879.

25. Ibid., March 6 and 20, April 3.

26. Ibid., March 13.

27. Ibid., April 3.

28. Ibid., April 10.

29. Ibid., April 17.

30. Boykin, *Georgia Baptists*, p. 67.

31. *The Christian Index*, March 20, 1890.

32. *The Cherokee Advance* (Canton), September 23, 1882; Brown Scrapbook, 1880–82, Joseph Emerson Brown Collection, University of Georgia Library.

33. "Minutes of the Southern Baptist Convention," vol. 3, 1880; vol. 2. 1883; 1884, pp. 2–9.

34. *Atlanta Constitution*, May 11, 1879.

35. *August Chronicle*, May 10, 1885; Brown Scrapbook, 1884–85, Joseph Emerson Brown Collection, University of Georgia Library. See also, "Minutes of The Southern Baptist Convention, 1885," pp. 30–34.

36. *Atlanta Constitution*, February 14, 1892.

37. Ibid., April 15, 1893; April 15, 1894.

38. Ibid., April 23, 1882.

39. Ibid., February 17, 1884.

40. Ibid., May 3, 1891.

41. Brown to Rush Brown, October 30, 1894, Joseph Emerson Brown Correspondence, Georgia State Department of Archives and History, Atlanta, Georgia.

42. *Atlanta Constitution*, December 1, 1894.

43. Ibid.

44. Ibid.

45. *Atlanta Journal*, December 1, 1894.

46. *Atlanta Constitution*, December 1, 1894.

47. *Senate Journal*, 1893, p. 312.

48. *Atlanta Constitution*, December 1, 1894.

49. *The Christian Index*, December 6, 1894.

50. Ibid.

Bibliography

MANUSCRIPTS

Alexander H. Stephens Papers. Emory University Library, Emory University, Georgia. More than 2,000 items.

Alexander H. Stephens Papers, 1844–1872. Brady Memorial Library, College of the Sacred Heart, Manhattanville, N. Y. 3,053 pieces of correspondence, mostly between A. H. Stephens and Linton Stephens.

Annals of Savannah, 1850–1937. "A Digest and Index of the Newspaper Record of Events and Opinions," Works Progress Administration, 87 volumes, 1937–1939. (Typescript).

Colonel David C. Barrow Papers. University of Georgia Library, Athens, Georgia.

Executive Letter Books of Governor Alfred H. Colquitt. Georgia State Department of Archives and History, Atlanta, Georgia.

"Executive Minutes of Georgia, 1865–1895." Georgia State Department of Archives and History, Atlanta, Georgia.

"Faculty Minutes of the University of Georgia, 1866–1895." University of Georgia Library, Athens, Georgia.

Felix Hargrett Collection of Joseph E. Brown Papers. University of Georgia Library, Athens, Georgia.

Howell Cobb Papers. University of Georgia Library, Athens, Georgia. A privately owned collection.

John B. Gordon Papers. Emory University Library, Emory University, Georgia. A small collection with a few Brown items.

John B. Gordon Papers. Georgia State Department of Archives and History, Atlanta, Georgia. A small collection of letters.

James B. Hambleton Collection. Emory University Library, Emory University, Georgia. Contains a few letters written by John B. Gordon about Georgia politics.

John Hill Hewitt Collection. Emory University Library, Emory University, Georgia.

Joseph Emerson and Elizabeth Gresham Brown Collection. University of Georgia Library, Athens, Georgia. Contains scrapbooks, clippings, family pictures, and a few manuscripts.

Joseph E. Brown Correspondence. Georgia State Department of Archives and History, Atlanta, Georgia. Mostly about Brown as governor.

Joseph E. Brown Correspondence. Emory University Library, Emory University, Georgia. Chiefly concerned with Brown's governorship.

Joseph M. Brown Papers. University of Georgia Library, Athens, Georgia. Three boxes of letters, some personal, written between 1860 and 1930.

Keith Read Manuscript Collection. University of Georgia Library, Athens, Georgia. Contains several letters written by Brown.

L. N. Trammell Collection. Emory University Library, Emory University, Georgia. Three folders of correspondence, some from Brown to Trammell.

"Minutes of the Georgia Baptist Convention, 1865–1894." Mercer University Library, Macon, Georgia. (On microfilm).

"Minutes of the Southern Baptist Convention, 1865–1894." Mercer University Library, Macon, Georgia. (On microfilm).

Private Letter Book of Governor Alfred H. Colquitt. Georgia State Department of Archives and History, Atlanta, Georgia. Personal letters of the Governor.

Rebecca Latimer Felton Papers. University of Georgia Library, Athens, Georgia. Contains a few letters from Brown to Dr. and Mrs. William H. Felton.

Telamon Cuyler Collection. University of Georgia Library, Athens, Georgia. An extensive collection of correspondence and documents of a governmental and political nature.

"Trustee Minutes of the University of Georgia, 1866–1894." University of Georgia Library, Athens, Georgia.

University of Georgia Trustees correspondence. University of Georgia Library, Athens, Georgia. A number of letters from Brown to the Trustees' secretary is in this collection.

Western and Atlantic Railroad Collection. University of Georgia Library, Athens, Georgia. Three small boxes of reports and pamphlets.

PUBLIC DOCUMENTS

Acts of the General Assembly of the State of Georgia. Atlanta: Various printers, 1865–1894.

Can a Negro Hold Office in Georgia? Arguments of Counsel with the Opinions of the Judges, and the Decision of the Court in the Case of Richard W. White, Clerk of Superior Court of Chatham County, Plaintiff in Error, versus the State of Georgia, ex relatione William J. Clements, Defendant in Error. Quo warranto. Chatham. Atlanta: Daily Intelligencer, 1869. 179 pages.

Candler, A. D., ed. *Confederate Records of the State of Georgia.* 5 vols. Atlanta: Charles P. Byrd, State Printer, 1909–1911.

Congressional Globe, Fortieth Congress, First Session, Part II, 1867. Washington, D. C.: F. J. Rives and George A. Bailey, 1868.

Congressional Record. Proceedings and Debates of the Congress of the United States. Washington, D. C.: United States Government Printing Office, 1880–1891.

Journal of the House of Representatives of the State of Georgia. Atlanta: Various printers, 1865–1894.

Journal of the Senate of the State of Georgia. Atlanta: Various printers, 1865–1894.

Lawyers Test Oath. United States District Court, Southern District of Georgia, May Term, 1866. Ex Parte William Law. Argument of Hon. Henry S. Fitch, United States District Attorney. Savannah: News and Herald Printers, 1866. 22 pages.

Lease of the Western & Atlantic Railroad. Act Authorizing Same,

*Together with Contract of Lease, Bond and Lessees and Inventory, and Report of Commissioners. Published for Use of the General Assembly, 1888.*Atlanta: W. J. Campbell, State Printer, 1888–1896.

Major General Meade's Report on the Ashburn Murder, Atlanta: n.p., 1868. 130 pages.

Majority and Minority Reports of the Joint Committee Appointed to Investigate the Fairness or Unfairness of the Contract Known as the Lease of the Western & Atlantic Railroad. n.p.:n.d. 47 pages.

Opinion of Honorable John Erskine, United States District Court of Georgia, in Ex Parte William Law, Decided May Term, 1866. Savannah: Republican Office, 1866. 29 pages.

Remarks and Statements on the Condition of the Western & Atlantic Before the Finance Committee of the House of Representatives, September 23, 1870. n.p.:n.d. 14 pages.

Report of the Tenth Census of the United States. Washington D. C.: United States Government Printing Office, 1881.

Report of the Commissioners, Viz: J.O.A. Clark, Jos. E. Brown, Benj. H. Hill, J.B. Gordon and David Wills, Appointed by His Excellency, James M. Smith, under a Resolution of the General Assembly, Approved March 2, 1874, "to perfect a plan for the affiliation, by mutual consent, of the University and the Denominational Colleges of Georgia." etc., to the General Assembly, through his Excellency, The Governor, at its session held in Atlanta, January 13, 1872. n.p.:n.d. 27 pages.

Report of the Committee of the Legislature to investigate the Bonds of the State of Georgia, Issued or Negotiated Since July 4, 1868. Atlanta: W. A. Hemphill, Public Printer, 1872. 184 pages.

Report of the Georgia General Assembly Committee on the Penitentiary in 1886. n.p.:n.d. 8 pages.

Report of the Joint Committee Appointed to Investigate into Certain Matters Pertaining to the Affairs and Present Condition of the Western & Atlantic Railroad. Atlanta: George W. Harrison, State Printer, 1887. 66 pages.

Report of the Joint Committee of the General Assembly of Georgia, Appointed to Investigate the Lease of the Western & Atlantic Railroad, 1880–1890. Atlanta: James P. Harrison and Company, Printers and Publishers, 1881. 171 pages.

Report of the Joint Committee to Investigate the Condition of the Western & Atlantic Railroad, Submitted to the Two Houses of the General

Assembly, Thursday, February 25, 1869. n.d.:n.p. 96 pages.

Report of Major General Meade's Military Operations and Administration of Civil Affairs in the Third Military District and Department of the South, for the Year 1868, With Accompanying Documents. Atlanta: Assistant Adjutant General's Office, Department of the South, 1868. 105 pages.

Report of the Majority of the Joint Committee Appointed by the General Assembly to Investigate the Fairness or Unfairness of the Contract known as the Lease of the Western & Atlantic Railroad Made December 27, 1870, by Rufus B. Bullock, Late Governor, and to investigate the Question of Fraud in said Contract, if any Exists. Atlanta: n.p., 1872.

Reports of Cases in Law and Equity Argued and Determined in the Supreme Court of Georgia. Atlanta: Harrison Company, 1867–1875.

Review of the Majority Report on the State Road Lease by B. H. Hill. Atlanta: W. R. Barrow, Book and General Job Printer, 1872. 31 pages.

Second Annual Report of the Officers of the Western & Atlantic Railroad Company, January 1, 1873. Atlanta: W. R. Barrow, Book and General Job Printer, 1872. 31 pages.

Testimony Before the Western & Atlantic Investigating Committee, Investigating the Western & Atlantic Railroad Lease. Atlanta: n.p., n.d. 310 pages.

The War of Rebellion: A Compilation of the Official Records of the Union and Confederate Armies. 3 ser., 129 vols., Washington D. C.: Government Printing Office, 1880–1901.

Western and Atlantic Railroad Lease. Betterments. Argument of Boykin Wright, Esq. of Counsel for Lessees, Before the Joint Committee of the General Assembly. What the Lessees Claim and What they do not Claim. Augusta: Chronicle, Printers and Stationers, 1888. 23 pages.

PAMPHLETS

Argument of E. B. Stahlman, Before the Joint Committee of the General Assembly. The Rights of the Lessees of the Western & Atlantic Railroad Company Under the Contract with the State of Georgia. Atlanta: Constitution Publishing Company, 1889. 29 pages.

Argument of Ex-Governor Joseph E. Brown, President of the Western & Atlantic Railroad Company, Before the Revision Committee of the Constitutional Convention, on the question of the Railroad Interests of Georgia, and More Especially on the Injuries that Would Result to the Railroads and the People from the Policy of Establishing Uniform Rates on all Freights over our Railroad Lines. Atlanta: Constitution Publishing Company, 1877. 29 pages.

Argument of Joseph E. Brown, President of the Western & Atlantic Railroad Company, Before the Joint Committee of the Georgia Legislature, on the Lease of the Western and Atlantic Railroad, and the Sufficiency of the Bond Given by Said Company. Atlanta: Constitution Publishing Company, 1881. 35 pages.

Argument of Joseph E. Brown, President of the Western & Atlantic Railroad Company, on the Question: 1st. Who are the Lessees of Said Road? 2nd. Does the Law Require that a Majority of the Lessees or the Shareholders Continue to Reside in the State of Georgia? 3rd. Has there been Discrimination? Atlanta: Constitution Publishing Company, 1881. 16 pages.

Argument of Julius L. Brown, Attorney for the Western & Atlantic Railroad Company, Before the Joint Judiciary Committee of the Legislature of Georgia, Convened in the Senate Chamber, Wednesday Afternoon, November 22, 1882. Upon the Resolutions of Senator Jones of the 43d District, and Mr. Brooks of Floyd, to Dismiss the Suit Brought by the State of Georgia Against the Western and Atlantic Railroad Company. Atlanta: Constitution Publishing Company, 1883. 34 pages.

Brown, Joseph E., *Letter from Hon. Joseph E. Brown to Governor John B. Gordon, in Reference to the State Road, in which the Rights and Liabilities of the Lessees and the Question of Betterments are Discussed.* Atlanta: Constitution Publishing Company, 1887. 14 pages.

Brown, Joseph E., *Letter from Joseph E. Brown, President of the Western & Atlantic Railroad on the Question: 1. Who are the lessees of said road? 2. Does the law require a majority of the lessees to continue to reside in Georgia? 3. Has there been discrimination?* Atlanta: Constitution Publishing Company, 1881. 16 pages.

Brown, Joseph E., *Letter from Joseph E. Brown, President of the Western & Atlantic Railroad Company on the Subject of the Settlement between the State and the Lessees on the Question of Betterments, Taxes, etc., Discussed, Arbitration Proposed.* Atlanta: W. J. Campbell, State Printer, 1887. 7 pages.

Comments on Governor Joseph E. Brown's Gift to the University of Georgia. Atlanta: Constitution Publishing Company, 1883. 35 pages.

Governor Brown and the Columbus Prisoners. n.p.:n.d. 16 pages. Contains newspaper clippings concerning the Brown–Garrard controversy.

Joseph E. Brown's Address on the Public Issues of the Country, to the People of Georgia at Macon, Georgia, October 23, 1890. Atlanta: Constitution Publishing Company, 1890. 23 pages.

Radical Rule: Military Outrage in Georgia. Arrest of Columbus Prisoners: With Facts Connected with Their Imprisonment and Release. Louisville: John P. Morton and Company, 1868. 199 pages.

Speech of Honorable Joseph E. Brown, of Georgia, Delivered in the Senate of the United States, April 14, 1881, A Free Ballot and a Fair Count. Washington, D.C.: n.p., 1881. 20 pages.

Speech of Honorable Joseph E. Brown, of Georgia, Delivered in the Senate of the United States, June 2, 1886, in Opposition to the Bankrupt Bill. Washington D.C.: n.p., 1886. 8 pages.

Speech of Honorable Joseph E. Brown, of Georgia, Delivered in the Senate of the United States, April 18, 1881, in Reply to the Republican Senators on the Right of the Majority to Rule. Washington, D.C.: n.p., 1881. 8 pages.

Speech of Honorable Joseph E. Brown, of Georgia, Delivered in the Senate of the United States, April 30, 1886., On the Amendment of the Postal-Appropriation bill, to encourage lines of American built steamers to carry the mail to Central and South America, and other countries; thereby opening lines of communication to enlarged commerce with those countries. Washington, D.C.: n.p., 1886. 15 pages.

Speech of Honorable Joseph E. Brown, of Georgia, Delivered in the Senate of the United States, December 14, 1882, On the Bill for Civil Service Reform. Washington, D.C.: n.p., 1882. 15 pages.

Speech of Honorable Joseph E. Brown, of Georgia, Delivered in the Senate of the United States, January 12, 1887. On the Interstate Commerce Bill as Reported by the Committee of Conference. Washington, D.C.: n.p., 1887. 7 pages.

Speech of Honorable Joseph E. Brown, of Georgia, Delivered on the 18th of March, 1886, in the Senate of the United States. On the President Alone Has the Power in His Discretion to Remove Federal Officers. Washington, D.C.: n.p., 1886. 18 pages.

Speech of Honorable Joseph E. Brown, of Georgia, Delivered in the Senate of the United States, March 14, 1888, On the Proper Mode of Collecting the Revenues of the United States. Washington, D.C.: n.p., 1888. 35 pages.

Speech of Honorable Joseph E. Brown, of Georgia, Delivered in the Senate of the United States on the 19th and 20th of February, 1883, On the Proper Rule for Raising the Revenue to Support the Government, and How the Burdens of the Tariff should be Distributed. Washington, D.C.: n.p., 1883. 15 pages.

Speech of Honorable Joseph E. Brown, of Georgia, Delivered in the Senate of the United States, January 14, 1886. On the Silver Question. Washington, D.C.: n.p., 1886. 16 pages.

Speech of Honorable Joseph E. Brown, of Georgia, Delivered in the Senate of the United States, on March 27, 1882. On the Tariff Commission Bill. Washington, D.C.: n.p., 1882. 16 pages.

Speech of Honorable Joseph E. Brown, of Georgia, Delivered in the Senate of the United States, January 25, 1887. On Woman Suffrage. Washington, D.C.: n.p., 1887. 15 pages.

Speech of Honorable Joseph E. Brown, of Georgia, in the Senate of the United States, January 16 and 17, 1885. General Remarks on Railroads. Competition and Pooling and the Carrying of Like Commodities a Longer Distance for Less Money Discussed. Washington, D.C.: n.p., 1885. 22 pages.

Speech of Honorable Joseph E. Brown, of Georgia, in the Senate of the United States, in Reply to Senator Morgan on the Educational Bill. Washington, D.C.: n.p., 1884. 16 pages.

Speech of Honorable Joseph E. Brown, of Georgia, in the Senate of the United States, March 25, 1884, On the Bill to Aid in the Establishment and Temporary Support of the Common Schools. Washington, D.C.: n.p., 1884. 13 pages.

Speech of Honorable Joseph E. Brown, of Georgia, in the United States Senate, Wednesday December 15, 1880. On the Educational Fund. Washington, D.C.: n.p., 1880. 13 pages.

Speech of Honorable Joseph E. Brown, of Georgia, in the Senate of the United States, June 26, 1884, On the Internal Revenue and the Whisky Monopoly. The Injustice of the System Discussed. It Ought to be Abolished. Washington, D.C.: n.p., 1884. 8 pages.

Speech of Honorable Joseph E. Brown, of Georgia, in the Senate of the United States, January 11, 1884. On the Mormon Question. Washington, D.C.: n.p., 1884. 24 pages.

Speech of Honorable Joseph E. Brown, of Georgia, in the Senate of the United States, May 27, 1884. Polygamy in Utah and New England contrasted. Washington, D.C.: n.p., 1884. 32 pages.

Speech of Honorable Joseph E. Brown, of Georgia, in the Senate of the United States, January 19 and 21, 1889. On the Question of the Proper Tariff on Rice. Washington, D.C.: n.p., 1889. 23 pages.

Speech of Honorable Joseph E. Brown, of Georgia, in the Senate of the United States. On the Tariff and Internal Revenue System. On Tuesday, January 23, 1883. Washington, D.C.: n.p., 1883. 15 pages.

Speech of Honorable Joseph E. Brown, of Georgia, in the Senate of the United States, June 20, 1888, On the Weil La Abra and Rebecca Claims. Washington, D.C.: n.p., 1888. 15 pages.

Speech of Honorable Joseph E. Brown, of Georgia. On the Mormon Question, Delivered in the Senate of the United States, on the 16th Day of February, 1882. Washington, D.C.: n.p., 1882. 15 pages.

Speech of Joseph E. Brown at Marietta, Georgia, March 18, 1868. n.p., 1868. 8 pages.

Many of these documents and pamphlets are found in the DeRenne Collection in the University of Georgia Library at Athens.

NEWSPAPERS

Atlanta Constitution, 1868–1895.
Atlanta Daily New Era, 1868.
Atlanta Intelligencer, 1865–1869.
Atlanta Journal, 1883–1895.
Atlanta Sun, 1872.
Augusta Chronicle, 1865–1890.
Augusta Constitutionalist, 1865–1867.

The Christian Index, 1865–1895.
Columbus Enquirer, 1865–1874.
Columbus Sun, 1865–1874.
Columbus Enquirer-Sun, 1874–1890.
Cordele Dispatch, 1955.
Elberton Gazette and New South, 1878–1884.
(Atlanta) *Georgia Weekly Opinion*, 1867–1868.
Milledgeville Confederate Union, 1865.
Milledgeville Federal Union, 1865–1870.
Savannah Daily Herald, 1865.
Savannah News, 1878–1894.
(Athens) *Southern Watchman*, 1870–1875.
Thomasville Southern-Enterprise, 1867–1870.

UNPUBLISHED THESES
AND DISSERTATIONS

Autry, Willie Mae (Stowe). "The International Cotton Exposition, Atlanta, Georgia, 1881." M.A. thesis, University of Georgia, Athens, Georgia, 1938.

Coleman, Kenneth. "The Gubernatorial Administration of Alfred H. Colquitt." M.A. thesis, University of Georgia, Athens, Georgia, 1940.

Speers, Leona. "The Senatorial Career of Joseph E. Brown." M.A. thesis, University of Georgia, Athens, Georgia, 1954.

Ward, Judson C. "Georgia Under the Bourbon Democrats, 1872–1890." Ph.D. dissertation, University of North Carolina, Chapel Hill, North Carolina, 1947. On microfilm in the University of Georgia Library at Athens, Georgia.

BOOKS

Arnett, Alex Mathews. *The Populist Movement in Georgia.* Columbia Studies in History, Economics and Public Law, no. 235. New York: Columbia University Press, 1922.

Avery, I W. *The History of Georgia from 1850 to 1881.* New York: Brown and Derby Publishing Company, 1881.

Bonner, James C., and Roberts, Lucien E., eds. *Studies in Georgia History.* Athens: University of Georgia Press, 1940.

Boykin, Samuel. *History of the Baptist Denomination in Georgia: With Biographical Compendium and Portrait Gallery of Baptist Ministers and Other Georgia Baptists.* Atlanta: James P. Harrison and Co., 1881.

Bryan, T. Conn. *Confederate Georgia.* Athens: University of Georgia Press, 1953.

Conway, Alan. *The Reconstruction of Georgia.* Minneapolis: University of Minnesota Press, 1966.

Coulter, E. Merton. *College Life in the Old South.* New York: Macmillan Co., 1928.

Coulter, E. Merton. *The Confederate States of America, 1861–1865.* History of the South, vol. 7. Baton Rouge: Louisiana State University Press, 1950.

Coulter, E. Merton. *Georgia, A Short History.* Chapel Hill: University of North Carolina Press, 1947.

Coulter, E. Merton. *The South During Reconstruction, 1865–1877.* History of the South, vol. 8. Baton Rouge: Louisiana State University Press, 1947.

Craven, Avery O. *The Growth of Southern Nationalism, 1848–1861.* History of the South, vol. 6. Baton Rouge: Louisiana State University Press, 1953.

Davis, William Watson. *The Civil War and Reconstruction in Florida.* Columbia Studies in History, Economics and Public Law, no. 131. New York: Columbia University Press, 1913.

Dorris, Jonathan T. *Pardon and Amnesty Under Lincoln and Johnson.* Chapel Hill: University of North Carolina Press, 1953.

Eckenrode, H. J.*Jefferson Davis.* New York: Macmillan Co., 1923.

Felton, Mrs. William H. *My Memoirs of Georgia Politics.* Atlanta: Index Printing Company, 1911.

Fielder, Herbert. *A Sketch of the Life and Times and Speeches of Joseph E. Brown.* Springfield, Mass.: Press of Springfield Printing Co., 1883.

Flippin, Percy Scott. *Herschal V. Johnson of Georgia: States Rights Unionist.* Richmond, Va.: Press of the Dietz Printing Co., 1931.

Franklin, John Hope. *The Militant South, 1800–1861.* Cambridge, Mass.: Harvard University Press, 1956.

Gordon, John B. *Reminiscences of the Civil War*. New York: Charles Scribner's Sons, 1904.

Grant, U. S. *Personal Memoirs of U. S. Grant*. 2 vol. New York: Charles L. Webster and Co., 1886.

Green, Fletcher M., ed. *Essays in Southern History Presented to Joseph Gregoire de Roulhac Hamilton*. James Sprunt Studies in History, vol. 31. Chapel Hill: University of North Carolina Press, 1949.

Joubert, William H. *Southern Freight Rates in Transition*. Gainesville: University of Florida Press, 1949.

Kirwan, Albert D., ed. *The Confederacy*. New York: Meridian Books, 1959.

Hill, Louise Biles. *Joseph E. Brown and the Confederacy*. Chapel Hill: University of North Carolina Press, 1939.

Hull, A. L. *A Historical Sketch of the University of Georgia*. Atlanta: Foote and Davies Co., 1894.

McCallie, S. W. *A Preliminary Report on the Mineral Resources of Georgia*. Atlanta: Stein Printing Co., 1926.

McGrane, Reginald C. *Foreign Bondholders and American Debts*. New York: Macmillan Co., 1935.

Mell, Patrick Hues, Jr. *The Life of Patrick Hues Mell*. Louisville: Baptist Publishing House., 1895.

Montgomery, Horace. *Cracker Parties*. Baton Rouge: Louisiana State University Press, 1950.

Mueller, William A. *A History of Southern Baptist Theological Seminary*. Nashville: Broadman Press, 1959.

Nixon, Raymond B. *Henry W. Grady, Spokesman of the New South*. New York: Alfred A. Knopf, 1943.

Northen, William J., ed. *Men of Mark in Georgia*. 7 vols. Atlanta: A. B. Caldwell, 1911.

Orr, Dorothy. *A History of Education in Georgia*. Chapel Hill: University of North Carolina Press, 1950.

Owsley, Frank L. *King Cotton Diplomacy*. 2nd ed. Chicago: University of Chicago Press, 1959.

Pearce, Haywood J., Jr. *Benjamin H. Hill: Secession and Reconstruction*. Chicago: University of Chicago Press, 1928.

Phillips, Ulrich B., ed. *The Correspondence of Robert Toombs,*

Alexander H. Stephens and Howell Cobb. Annual Report of the American Historical Association for the year 1911. vol. 2. Washington, D. C.: United States Government Printing Office, 1913.

Phillips, Ulrich B. *The Life of Robert Toombs.* New York: Macmillan Co., 1913.

Poor, Henry V. *Manual of the Railroads of the United States.* New York: H. V. and H. W. Poor, 1869–(published annually).

Ragsdale, B. D. *The Story of Georgia Baptists.* 3 vols. Macon Ga.: Author and Mercer University, 1935.

Randall, J. G. *The Civil War and Reconstruction.* New York: D. C. Heath and Co., 1953.

Richardson, E. Ramsay. *Little Aleck: The Fighting Vice-President of the Confederacy.* Indianapolis: Bobbs-Merrill Co., 1932.

Saye, Albert B. *A Constitutional History of Georgia, 1732–1945.* Athens: University of Georgia Press, 1948.

Scott, William A., *The Repudiation of State Debts: A Study in the Financial History of Mississippi, Florida, Alabama, North Carolina, South Carolina, Georgia, Louisiana, Arkansas, Tennessee, Minnesota, Michigan and Virginia.* New York: Thomas Y. Crowell and Co., 1893.

Stevens, O. B. and Wright, R. F. *Georgia, Historical and Industrial.* Atlanta: Georgia Department of Agriculture, 1901.

Stovall, Pleasant A. *Robert Toombs, Statesman, Speaker, Soldier, Sage.* New York: Cassell Publishing Co., 1929.

Talmadge, John E. *Rebecca Latimer Felton: Nine Stormy Decades.* Athens: University of Georgia Press, 1960.

Tankersly, Allen P. *John B. Gordon: A Study in Gallantry.* Atlanta: Whitehall Press, 1955.

Telfair, Nancy. *A History of Columbus, Georgia, 1828–1928.* Columbus, Ga.: Historical Publishing Co., 1929.

Thompson, C. Mildred. *Reconstruction in Georgia.* New York: Columbia University Press, 1915.

Tuck, Henry C. *Four Years at the University of Georgia.* Athens, Ga.: Author, 1938.

Von Abele, Rudolph. *Alexander H. Stephens, A Biography.* New York: Alfred A. Knopf, 1946.

Waddell, James D., ed. *Biographical Sketch of Linton Stephens.* Atlanta: Dodson and Scott, 1877.

Wiley, Bell Irvin. *The Life of Johnny Reb: The Common Soldier of the Confederacy.* New York: Bobbs-Merrill Co., 1943.

Wiley, Bell Irvin. *Southern Negroes, 1861–1865.* New York: Rinehart and Co., 1953.

Woodward, C. Vann. *Origins of the New South, 1877–1913.* History of the South, vol. 9. Baton Rouge: Louisiana State University Press, 1951.

Woodward, C. Vann. *Tom Watson, Agrarian Rebel.* New York: Macmillan Co., 1938.

Woolley, Edwin C. *The Reconstruction of Georgia.* New York: Columbia University Press, 1901.

ARTICLES IN PERIODICALS

Lawrence, Alexander A. "Henry Kent McCay, Forgotten Jurist." *Georgia Bar Journal* 9 (August, 1949): 17.

Phillips, Ulrich B. "An American State-Owned Railroad." *Yale Review* 15 (November, 1906): 256–82,

Roberts, Derrell C. "Joseph E. Brown and the Atlanta Public Schools." *Peabody Journal of Education* 43 (July, 1965): 42–49.

Roberts, Derrell C. "Joseph E. Brown and His Atlanta Real Estate." *The Atlanta Historical Bulletin* 15 (Summer, 1970): 43–48.

Roberts, Derrell C. "Joseph E. Brown: Baptist Layman." *The* (Baptist) *Quarterly Review* 25 (First Quarter, 1965): 67–72.

Roberts, Derrell C. "Joseph E. Brown and The Convict Leave System." *The Georgia Historical Quarterly* 44 (December, 1960): 399–410.

Roberts, Derrell C. "Joseph E. Brown and the Failure of Atlanta's Citizen's Bank." *The Atlanta Historical Bulletin* 13 (December, 1968): 42–45.

Roberts, Derrell C. "Joseph E. Brown and The Florida Election of 1876." *The Florida Historical Quarterly* 40 (January, 1962): 217–25.

Roberts, Derrell C. "Joseph E. Brown and His Georgia Mines." *The Georgia Historical Quarterly* 52 (September, 1968): 285–92.

Roberts, Derrell C. "Joseph E. Brown and The University of Georgia." *The Georgia Review* 19 (Summer, 1965): 239–49.

Small, Sam W. "The Constitutional Convention of 1877." *Report of the Forty-Fourth Annual Session of the Georgia Bar Association* (1927): 251–52.

Spalding, Mrs. John S. "The Second Baptist Church." *Atlanta Historical Bulletin* 8, no. 30 (October, 1945): 37–38.

Taylor, Elizabeth. "The Origins and Development of the Convict Lease System in Georgia." *Georgia Historical Quarterly* 26 (March, 1942): 113–28.

Woodward, C. Vann. "Bourbonism in Georgia." *North Carolina Historical Review* 16, no. 1 (January, 1939): 23–35.

Index

Adams–Clay Bargain, 86
Agriculture, 94–95
Akin, Warren, 9
American Party, 6, 7, 9
Andersonville Prison, 31, 32
Anzeiger des Westen, 54
Argo, 32
Ashburn, G. W., 52, 60, 75, 84
Athens Southern Banner, 58
Atkinson, William Y., 108
Atlanta, 29, 34, 35–36, 54, 57, 64,
73, 79, 81, 83, 85, 89, 92, 101,
102, 103, 105; bar, 66; Board
of Education, 97; business-
men, 44; people of, celebrate
defeat of Brown, 58; people
of, celebrate so-called Til-
den victory, 84; City Council,
97; Federal occupation of,
22; General Pope and, 48;
Brown's law practice in, 33, 41,
60; Brown family moves to,
100; railroad, 24, 91; Second
Baptist Church of, 103
Atlanta Constitution, 58–59, 62,
63, 71, 72, 75, 77, 79, 81, 87,
88, 106–107
Atlanta Intelligencer, 46

Atlanta Journal, 107
Augur, Major General Chris-
topher, 27
Augusta Arsenal, 14
Augusta Chronicle and Sentinel, 35,
47–48, 49, 77
Augusta Constitutionalist, 5
Austell, Alfred, 76
Avery, I. W., 71, 72, 106
Banks, 7
Baptist, 4, 76, 77, 97, 98, 103–106
Barrow, Benjamin, 77
Barrow, David C., 77
Bayard, Lt. William, 29
Bell, John, 22
Benning, General Henry L., 61
Betterments, 93–94
Blair, Francis P., Jr., 55
Blodgett, Foster, 57–58, 91
Bonds, Repudiation of State, 77
Brantly, Reverend W. T., 59, 104
Breckinridge, John C., 12
Brown Ancestry, 1
Brown, B. Gratz, 74–75
Brown, Charles McDonald, 102
Brown, Charles McDonald
Scholarship Fund, 96
Brown, Elijah A., 102

Brown, Elizabeth Gresham (Mrs. J. E.), 31, 101

Brown, Franklin Pierce, 5, 102–103

Brown, George M., 100

Brown, John Young, 86

Brown, Joseph, Grandfather Joseph E., 2

Brown, Joseph E.; 1; addresses Republican National Convention, 53; amnesty oath, 35; answers Garrard, 63; arrested, 27; arrival in Washington, 29; Baptist, 103–104; birth, 2; Bullock inauguration, 56; calling legislature, 30, 31; candidate for U. S. Senate, 1868, 57–58; changes position on War., 30, 31; Chief Justice, Georgia Supreme Court, 65–69; Constitutional Convention, 1868, 50; Convention, 1860, 11; corresponds with President Johnson, 34–35; death, 107; donation to University of Georgia, 96; Economics and Reconstruction, 50–51; elected Governor, 1861, 15; elected Governor, 1863, 15; election 1860, 12; election of 1876, 80–90; Electoral Commission, 86–87; end of Governorship, 24; family life, 100–103; Fanny Martin incident, 59; final relief of disabilities, 52; for Governor, 89; full pardon and amnesty granted, 35; funeral, 108; Jenkins for Governor, 37; Georgia Constitutional Convention, 1877, 87–88; Governor, 96; Governor candidate, 5; Governor nominee, 5; Governor, parole, 28; Governor's race in Georgia, 1868, 55–56; Howell Cobb, 18; illness, 32, 106–107; in U. S. Senate, 98–99; investigation of administration, 39–40; law practice, 41–42; leasing company, 92; legal profession, 60–69; letter on Reconstruction, 44–45; letter to the people, 12; letter to President Johnson, 29, 30; letter to President Johnson, 30, 31; liberal Republican, 73–75; Mitchell Heirs Case, 75; National Campaign, 1868, 55; Negroes holding office, 68; Negro question, 40–41; Notes on the Situation, 49; on divorce, 106; on Republicans, 87; opposed by ("Troup" pseudonym), 20; overthrow of Bullock, 73; parole, 25, 31; parole of honor, 31; President Atlanta Board of Education, 97–98; President Jefferson Davis, 18; President Johnson, 36; proposed duel with Toombs, 76–77; Reconstruction in Georgia, 34–35; Reconstruction policy, 52; resignation, 33; results of investigation of Governorship, 39–40; return from prison, 33; secession, 13; secession Convention, 13; second military Reconstruction, 71–72; Sherman, 22; speaks at Milledgeville, 47; speaks in Atlanta, 57; speaks in Savannah, 46; speaks to Georgia General Assembly, 22; speech on freed Negroes, 55–56; Stephens as United States Senator, 38–39; Stephens for Governor, 1865, 38; surrender, 25; surrenders Georgia Militia, 23; talks to President Johnson, 43;

to Washington, 43; trip to Washington, 29; University of Georgia Trustee, 96; U. S. Senate, 110–111; U. S. Senate candidate, 89; visits President Johnson, 29, 30; William Law Case, 41–42; witness against Davis, 29; wrote to President Johnson, 26
Brown, Joseph M. 102
Brown, Joseph M., Governor, 102
Brown, Julius, 101–102, 107
Brown, Mackey, 2
Brown, Mary Virginia, 102
Brown, Sally Eugenia, 102
Brownlow, Governor William G., 29, 56
Bryant, J. E., 73
Buchanan, President James, 6, 9
Bullock, Rufus B., 55, 56, 57, 58, 62, 65, 67, 68, 69, 72, 73, 77, 91–92
Calhoun Academy, 2
Camden, Battle, 2
Cameron, Simeon, 92
Carroll, General William, 2
Carroll Prison, 29, 31
Chandler, W. E., 82
Cherokee Baptist Railroad, 8
Christian Index, 104–105
Cincinnati Platform, 9, 12
Citizen's Bank, 102
Civil Rights, 78–79
Civil War, 15, 24, 103, 108–109
Clarke, E. Y., 84
Clements, William J., 67–68
Cleveland, Grover, 106
Clothing seized, 17
Coal, 94
Cobb, Howell, 6, 8, 9, 11, 13, 15, 18, 20, 57
Cobb, Thomas R. R., 12, 18
Colquitt, Alfred H., 4, 6, 88, 89–90, 98

Columbus Enquirer, 37
Columbus Prisoners, 60–65
Columbus Sun, 75
Compromise of 1850, 4, 10
Compromise of 1877, 89
Confederacy, 12, 14, 15, 18, 21, 24, 46, 48, 49, 50, 79
Confederate Bonds, 21
Confederate confiscation, 21
Confederate Congress, 20
Confederate Government, 19
Confederate soldiers, Georgia, 17
Confederate tax, 21
Congressional Reconstruction, 43
Conley, Benjamin, 73
Connally, Dr. E. L., 87, 88, 102
Conscription Act, 18–20, 49
Constitutional Convention, Georgia, 1865, 36
Constitutional Convention, Georgia, 1867–68, 50
Convict labor, 94
Conway, Thomas W., 53
Crawford, Martin, J., 61
Crisp, Charles F., 108
Dade County Coal Company, 94, 102
Davis, Jefferson, 18, 19, 21, 22, 23, 24, 29, 53
Dean, Reverend Charles P., 103
Delano, Columbus, 89, 92
Delano, John S., 92
Democrat, 58, 79, 80–89, 95–96, 98, 106
Democratic National Convention, 9, 100
Democratic National Convention, 1860, 11
Democratic National Convention, 1868, 54
Democratic Party, 44, 49, 52–53, 74, 78
Depression 1857, 7

Divorce, 106
Douglas, Stephen A., 10, 12
Dred Scott Decision, 12
Drew, George F., 82, 85
Duel, Toombs and Brown, 76–77
Duke, William, 62
Dumble, J. B., 37, 38
Dunn, General William M., 62
Edge, John M., 4
Education, 96–98, 111; and the Bible, 98
Election of 1852, 4
Election of 1859, 9
Electoral Commission, 85–87
Eleventh Amendment, 77
Erskine, John, 41, 42, 59, 70
Ex parte Garland, 41
Fairbanks, Charles, 84
Farm Credit, 95
Federal Arsenals, 17
Federal Troups, 20
Fifteenth Amendment, 70, 72
Fitch, Henry S., 41
Floyd, John B., Secretary of War, 13, 14
Foreign Relations Committee, 99
Fort Donelson, 17
Fort Pulaski, 14
Fort Warren, 38
Foster, Charles, 86
Fourteenth Amendment, 45, 50
Freedmen, 44
Froebel, B. W., 99
Fugitive Slave Laws, 14
Furlow, Timothy, 15
Gardner, James, 5
Garrard, Louis F., 62–65
Gartrell, L. J., 61
General Assembly, Georgia, 14, 28, 67, 68, 77, 91, 96
Georgia Baptist Convention, 104
Georgia Bar Association, 3, 66
Georgia, Financial Condition, 30
Georgia General Assembly, 21, 22, 75
Georgia Legislature, 12, 25, 26

Georgia Military Institute, 13
Georgia Militia, 13, 14, 20, 25
Georgia Platform, 10
Georgia Railroad Commission, 102
Georgia State Capitol, 108
Georgia Supreme Court, 60, 65–69, 75
Gordon, John B., 56, 86, 86–87, 89, 98
Grady, Henry W., 48, 81, 82, 83, 85
Grange, 95
Grant, U. S., 27, 28, 46, 54, 54–55, 56, 60, 62, 65, 80, 92
Greeley, Horace, 74–75
Gresham, Elizabeth (Mrs. J. E. Brown), 3
Griffin Daily News, 76
Habeas corpus, 18, 21
Hampton, Wade, 54
Hayes, Rutherford B., 80, 83, 85
Hewitt, Abram S., 81
Hill, Benjamin H., 6, 9, 12, 13, 23, 47–50, 52, 75, 89, 92
Hill, David B., 106
Hill, Joshua, 15, 22, 38–39, 57–58, 58
Hood, General John B., 20, 22
Howell, E. P., 87
Hulbert, E., 44
Hull, John L., 74–75
Hunnicutt, James W., 47
Jenkins, Charles J., 37, 39, 46
Joe Brown's Pets, 20
Joe Brown's Pikes, 17, 18
Johnson, Hershel V., 7, 12, 38–39
Johnson, James, 35, 36, 38–39, 89
Johnson, President Andrew, 26, 27, 29, 30, 31, 33–34, 35, 36, 38–39, 43, 54
Johnston, General Joseph E., 20, 24, 25, 30
Jordan, Charles L., 39

Kansas–Nebraska Bill, 6, 10
Kent, Alec, 107
Kerfoot, Reverend F. H., 108
Kimball, H. I., 76
King, William, 22
Kneeland, Captain, 27
Know-Nothing Party, 49
Ku Klux Klan, 70
Labor Committee, 99
Lamar, H. G., 5
Law of Nations, 41–42
Law practice, 100
Law, William, 41
Lawton, A. R., 98
Layman, 104–105
Lee, General Robert E., 24, 25, 30
Letcher, Governor John, 29
Leverett, Wesley, 2
Lewis, Dr. John W., 2, 8
Liberal Republican, 79, 89
Lincoln, Abraham, 12, 29, 20
Liquor restrictions, 15, 16
Lochrane, O. A., 37, 38, 39, 75–76
Louisville Journal, 54
Louisville & Nashville Railroad, 98
Lumpkin, John H., 5, 8
Lumpkin, Joseph Henry, 66
Macon Telegraph, 4, 20, 21
Martin, Fanny, 59
Mathews, Stanley, 86
Mayer, David, 32
McDonald, Henry, 108
McKay, H. K., 66, 67
Meade, General George G., 56, 61–65
Mell, Patrick Hues, 105
Mercer University, 96, 97
Military Commission, 61
Military occupation of the South, 43
Military preparation, 13
Milledgeville Federal Union, 45, 48
Miller, A. J., 4

Miller, H. V. M., 58
Mills, Captain, 84
Mitchell Heirs Case, 75
Mitchell, Samuel, 75
Morgan, Governor E. D. of New York, 14
Moses, R. J., 61, 66
Munitions, 17
Nashville, Chattanooga, and St. Louis Railroad, 93
Nashville Convention, 4
Negroes, 20, 40, 44, 47, 50, 54, 55, 57, 66–68, 70, 72, 78–79, 95, 97 98
New Orleans Democrat, 87
New South Concept, 108–111
New York Herald, 43, 81
Nichols, John C., 76
Nisbet, E. A., 15
Northern Baptists, 105
Norwood, Thomas M., 89
"Notes on the Situation," 47–48
Old South Concept, 108–109
Olmstead, Dr. J. C., 107
Opposition Party, 9
O'Reilly, Father, 103
Oglethorpe University, 102
Orphanage, 104
Peck, John B., 64
People's Party, 95–96
Phillips, General William, 63
Pierce, Franklin, 4
Polk, James K., 5
Pooling, 93
Pope, General John B., 48, 96
Populist Party, 95–96
Provost Marshall, 29
Public Schools, 8, 9
Radicals, 50
Radical Party, 44
Radical Reconstruction, 50
Randolph, George W., Secretary of War, 19, 20
Reconstruction Acts, 63, 68
Redding, A. W., 14

Republican, 12, 58, 66, 79, 80–90, 95–96, 98
Republican Convention, National, 53
Republican Convention of Georgia, 53
Republicans, Liberal, 73–75
Republican Party, 49, 52
"Review of Notes on the Situation," 49
Rising Fawn Iron Company, 95
Saffold, Thomas, P., 39
Salt, 15
Savannah Daily Herald, 28, 29
Schofield, General John M., 61, 65
Schurz, Carl, 53
Scrap iron, 8
Seago, A. K., 44
Secession, 12, 44
Second Baptist Church, 103, 105, 108
Selma (Alabama) *Times,* 62
Semmes, General Paul J., 14
Senate, Georgia State, 4
Seward, William H., Secretary of State, 35
Seymour, Horatio, 54–55, 56
Sherman, General William T., 20, 22, 24, 25, 30
Sherman, John, 52
Silliman, Professor Benjamin, 3
Silver, 98
Slavery, 13
Smith, James M., 73, 74–75, 89
Sons of Temperance, 4
Southern Baptist Convention, 105–106
Southern Baptist Theological Seminary, 97, 105, 108
Southern Pacific Railroad, 86
Spalding, A. T., 108
Specie payment, 7
Standard gauge, 92
Stanton, Edwin M., 26, 27, 28, 29

Starnes, E., 39
State Penitentiary, 17
States rights, 4
Stearns, Marcellus, 82
Stephens, Alexander H., 15, 24, 41, 42, 47, 57, 58, 68, 70, 73, 99, 103, 104, 106; candidate for Governor, 1865, 37–38; Columbus prisoners, 61, 64–65; Democratic convention, 1860, 11; habeas corpus, 21; imprisonment, 35, 36; lease of Western & Atlantic Railroad, 92; peace movement, 22; secession, 12, 13
Stephens, Linton, 6, 15, 21, 35, 38, 73, 300
Stiles, W. H., 5
Styles, Carey W., 58, 59, 64, 79
Sumner, Charles, 66
Supreme Court, Georgia, 91
Supreme Court, U. S., 70
Terry, General Alfred H., 68, 72, 76
Test Oath Act, 1862, 41
Test Oaths, 42, 55, 60
Texas & Pacific Railroad, 59
Thomas, General George H., 34
Tift, Nelson, 70, 72
Tilden, Samuel J., 80, 81, 82, 83, 84, 85, 86, 87
Toombs, Robert, 6, 12, 13, 15, 22, 47, 58, 73, 75, 76, 77, 96
Trammell, L. N., 3, 5, 65, 84, 88
Triumvirate, 89
United States Army, 1, 24
United States Congress, 47, 49, 71
United States Senate, 38, 52, 86–87, 89, 91, 98–99
United States Supreme Court, 41, 46, 60
University of Georgia, 77, 96, 102, 105
Van Buren, Martin, 106

Vance, Zebulon B., 29, 30
Virginia and Kentucky Resolutions, 53
Volunteers, 14
Wade, Benjamin, 66
Waitzfelder, Brothers, 39, 76, 109
Walker, Dawson, 43, 44, 55
Walker Iron and Coal Company, 94
Walker, Robert J., 6
Wallace, Campbell, 64
Ward, John E., 39
War relief, 16
Warner, Hiram, 5, 66, 68, 69

Western & Atlantic Railroad, 4, 6, 8, 9, 24, 25, 59, 64, 69, 71, 72, 75, 91–94, 102
Westmoreland, Dr. J. G., 102
Whitaker, J. I., 59
White vs. Clements, 67–68
White, Richard W., 67–68
Wilson, General J. H., 24, 25, 26, 27, 29, 34
Woman's Bill, 4
Women's Property Rights, 4
Wright, A. R., 68
Wright, R. K., 22
Yancey, William L., 11
Young, P. M. B., 81